COOL TOKYO GUIDE

ADVENTURES IN THE CITY OF KAWAII FASHION, TRAIN SUSHI AND GODZILLA

ABBY DENSON

TUTTLE Publishing

Tokyo | Rutland, Vermont | Singapore

ACKNOWLEDGMENTS

This book is dedicated to Matt Loux and Yuuko Koyama.
Thanks for sharing so many great adventures with me!

Extra special thanks go to Christopher Butcher, Andrew Woodrow-Butcher, Cindy Howle and Mayumi Abuku for their invaluable assistance with the production of this book.

My deepest gratitude goes out to all of my family members and friends for their support.

My heartfelt appreciation goes out to Fusami Ogi, Mika Sakki, Kaneko Atsushi, Yoko Oikawa, Youri Morinaga, Aloha Higa, Yoshiki Takahashi, Utomaru, Miyako Kojima, Norman England, and the many others who have always made me feel welcome during my travels. See you again soon!

CONTENTS

INTRODUCTION

Welcome to Cool Tokyo Guide!

I'm an American cartoonist who has had a longtime fascination with Japan, ever since I started reading manga and watching anime when I was a teen. While in college, I got the opportunity to study in Tokyo, where I met my friend Yuuko Koyama, a fellow cartoonist. We've since had many adventures together!

Perhaps you've read my previous travel book, Cool Japan Guide. In Cool Tokyo Guide I focus on, well, Tokyo. This book brings you more tips and recommendations from me, my husband Matt, friend Yuuko, and our cartoon cat friend, Kitty Sweet Tooth, and we hope you'll have fun touring the city with us.

One thing I've picked up over my years of traveling is that you must be prepared to research, to make mistakes, and to perhaps even look foolish sometimes. It's okay! That's how you learn, and I've found the people of Japan can be very welcoming and eager to assist when they are asked for help.

I remember the first time I visited Tokyo, back in 1997, when I was there to study at Sophia University's summer session. I was struck by how Tokyo was like New York City in many ways, but more so. More buildings, more people, more parks, and so many exciting things to see, do, and eat. It can be truly overwhelming (in a great way). At the same time, Tokyo's cleanliness, conveniences, and cultural differences can somehow make it all seem more manageable. As a frequent visitor to Tokyo, I'm excited to share my experiences and help you through some of the common pitfalls or culture-shock moments that you might encounter.

Just remember: don't miss the last train!

PRONUNCIATION GUIDE

At the start of each chapter Kitty Sweet Tooth will teach you some useful words and phrases. Here are a few basic rules of pronunciation.

In Japanese:

a is pronounced as in the word father

e is pronounced as in the word set

i is pronounced ee, as in the word seed

o is pronounced as in the word tote

u is pronounced oo, as in the word soon

Most consonants are pronounced as in English. G is always hard, as in goat. F is a softer sound than in English, so try not to let your teeth touch your bottom lip when pronouncing it.

R is also a softer sound, like a gentle curl/roll of the tongue.

There is no l, q, v or x sound in Japanese.

Let's learn new words with Kitty Sweet Tooth!

Chapter 1 introduces you to:

Sakura - cherry blossoms
Hanami - blossom viewing party
Matsuri - festival
Yatai - food stalls
Mikoshi - portable shrine
Hanabi - fireworks
Momijigari - leaf peeping
Kimono - traditional robelike garment
Kumade - rake
Shinkansen - bullet train

CHAPTER 1

We're going to Tokyo! Now what?

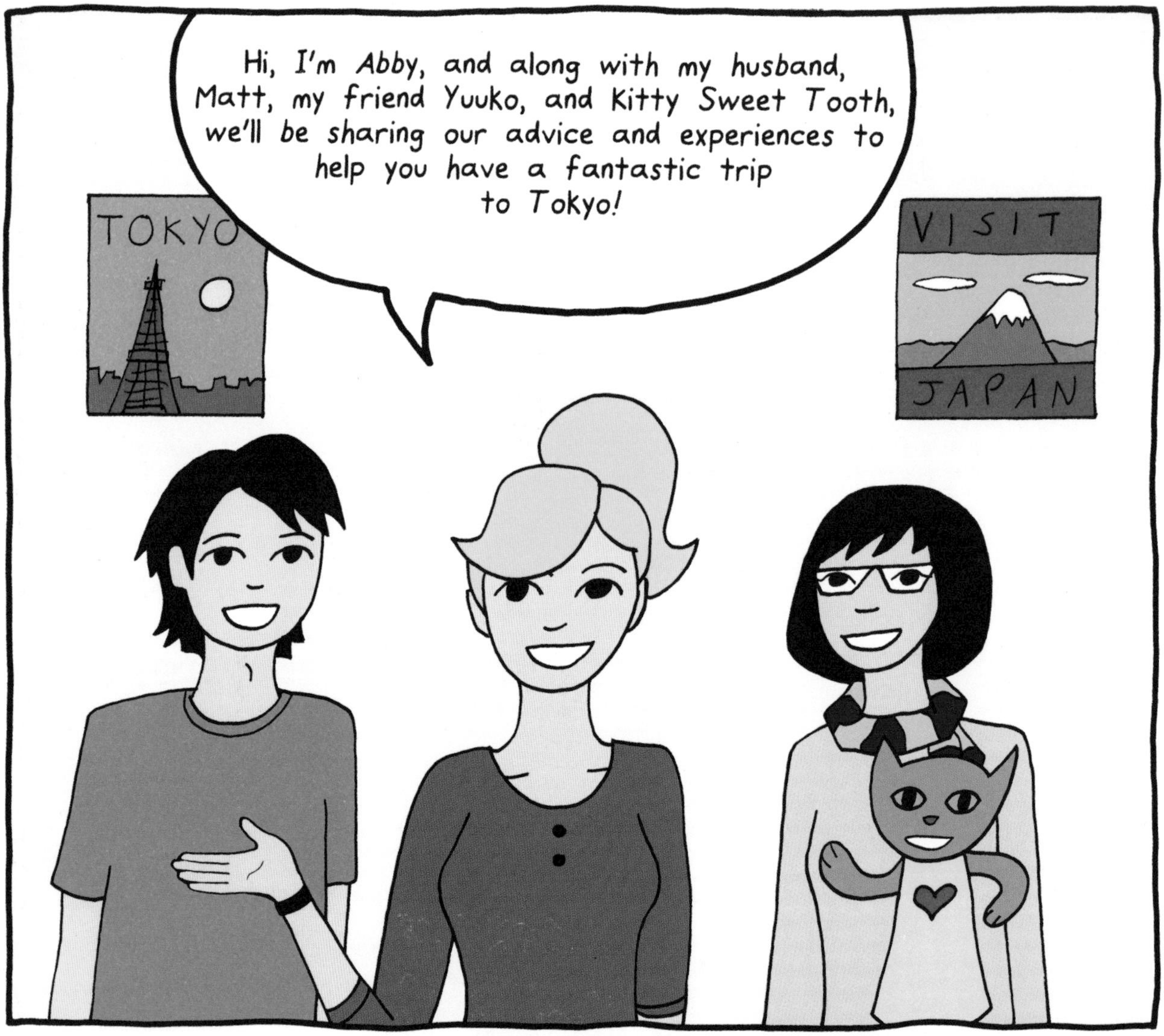
Hi, I'm Abby, and along with my husband, Matt, my friend Yuuko, and Kitty Sweet Tooth, we'll be sharing our advice and experiences to help you have a fantastic trip to Tokyo!
TOKYO
VISIT JAPAN

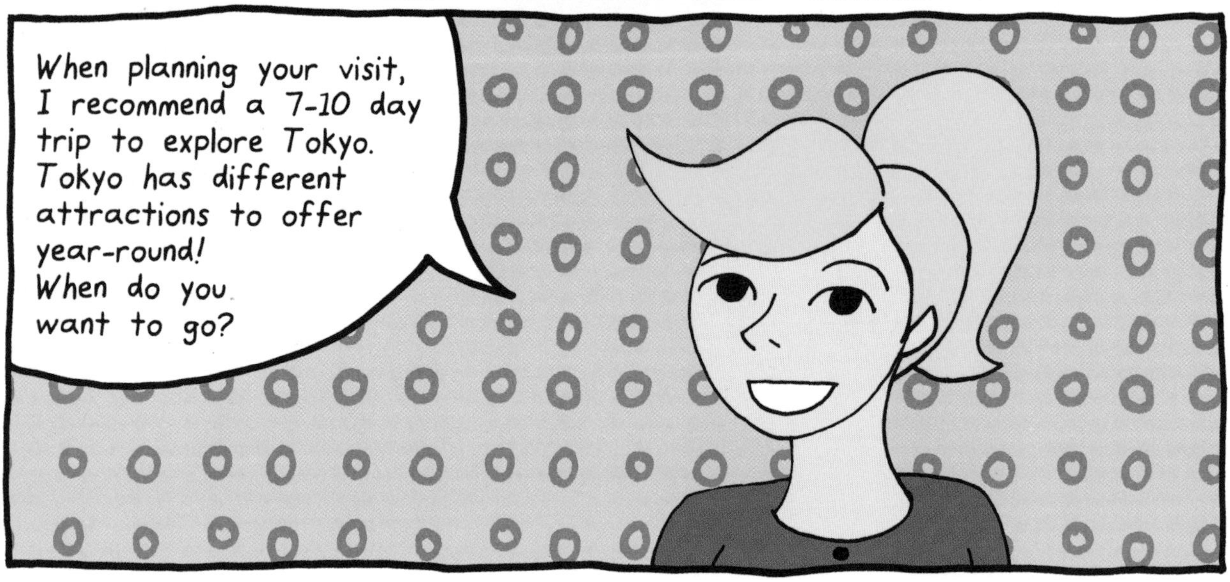
When planning your visit, I recommend a 7-10 day trip to explore Tokyo. Tokyo has different attractions to offer year-round! When do you want to go?

The most popular time to visit Tokyo is springtime, to experience the gorgeous blooms of the cherry blossoms (sakura). The weather is pleasant and sakura viewing parties (hanami) are a popular activity. It's a chance for friends to picnic in parks together and enjoy nature while drinking and socializing. Enjoying the fleeting beauty of sakura blooms is a favorite national pastime. The peak bloom lasts about a week (depending on weather conditions), and typically occurs mid to late April.

We especially enjoyed viewing the illuminated blossoms at night during the Nakameguro Sakura Festival, on the Meguro River. The views were gorgeous and vendors sold delicious food and drinks from their food stalls (yatai)!

Gorgeous!

Since Tokyo's climate is subtropical, the summer season is very hot, rainy, and humid, so be prepared for that! If you want to see summer festivals (matsuri) and fireworks (hanabi), summer could be your preferred time to visit. Sanno Matsuri is one of the biggest festivals to see in June.

Wow, what a lovely mikoshi!

It's also a good time to enjoy rooftop beer gardens!

Frozen beer!

In the summertime, firefly festivals are held to enjoy viewing the glowing insects in the night. You can find these at Mount Takao, Yomiuri Land, and in Setagaya Ward.

Wow, look at them glow!

One of my favorite times to visit is autumn, as the weather is cool and comfortable. The changing leaves are gorgeous, and at Rikugien Gardens they illuminate the colorful leaves for evening viewing! Viewing the changing autumn leaves is called momijigari.

In autumn you can also experience the festivals of Shichi-Go-San and Tori-no-Ichi. Shichi-Go-San is a Shinto festival where children of three, five, and seven years old are dressed in gorgeous kimonos and blessed at shrines. It's a great time to visit shrines and usually the children are happy to pose for photos in their finery.

11

Tori-no-Ichi is the "Rooster Market" held during days of the rooster on the traditional calendar in November at shrines and temples. Beautifully decorated bamboo rakes (kumade) are sold by vendors at many stands. They are believed to "rake in" good luck!

Traditionally, people bring back their old kumade from the previous year and buy new ones for the following year. Kumade are available in a huge range of designs and prices. Small ones can be quite affordable ($5-$10).

↖
One of the kumade we got.

Various yatai can also be enjoyed as part of the lively atmosphere late into the night. Ootori Jinja Shrine and Chokokuji Temple in Asakusa are popular places to experience Tori-no-Ichi. We attended the festival with our friend Yoshiki at Hanazono Shrine in Shinjuku.

Thanks for bringing us here!

This is so much fun!

Winter weather in Tokyo is generally mild and the city lights up with gorgeous holiday illuminations.

Galaxy Dome at Tokyo Dome City

Christmas is a romantic date night and Christmas cakes (strawberry shortcake) are everywhere.

Merry Christmas!

Thanks, Matt!

You'll also see KFC party barrels advertised, which are reserved in advance. Kentucky Fried Chicken is popular for Christmas meals!

One party barrel, please!

パーティバーレル

¥3880

Time to pack! I'm a fan of packing as lightly as possible (especially if you want to save room for souvenirs). The number one thing you must always remember to pack is any prescription medication you may have. Be sure to pack it in your carry-on bag. Prescription meds are the only things that might be difficult to replace in Tokyo. Also, get your flu shot before the trip if possible. It's no fun to get sick on vacation!

I recommend preparing a toiletry bag that has what you need, and just have it at the ready for any trip that comes up.

Clothes and toiletries are easy to find - just make sure you don't forget any medications!

I usually include an empty foldable bag or duffel bag in my hard shell roller suitcase and then put my clothes in the foldable bag and check that on the flight home. The more delicate souvenirs then go into the hard shell case. You can also buy more bags or luggage in Tokyo at stores like Don Quijote or Tokyu Hands.

hard shell

foldable duffle bag

cloth tote or Eco bag

Communication, Transportation, and Cash!

Most smartphones can be used in Japan; check with your provider if your SIM card is compatible, and research their plans for international data usage. Alternatively, you can rent a Wi-Fi hotspot or Japanese phone. Those can be found at airports in Japan. The Tabimori App is also especially helpful. Free Wi-Fi is now more available than ever in Japan, so check out JNTO's website for info. http://www.jnto.go.jp/eng/

Transportation in Tokyo is very easy! Trains can take you anywhere you want to go and usually there is English signage for them. When arriving via Narita or Haneda Airport, there are plenty of options for traveling into the city. Just purchase train or bus tickets after exiting the luggage pickup at the airport. You can explore all of the options beforehand at the airport websites:

http://www.narita-airport.jp/en
https://www.tokyo-airport-bldg.co.jp/en/

Accessing cash in Tokyo is easier than ever before! It's also very important, as many places don't accept credit card payment. 7-Eleven stores have international ATMs (as well as free Wi-Fi). Post offices have JP bank ATMs, just look for this red post office symbol.

Tokyo Tourist Information Centers are also convenient places to get cash and rent Wi-Fi hotspots, as well as buy tickets and make reservations for attractions.

http://www.his-j.com/japan-tourist/tyo/

Look for the "English" button first!

Before you travel to Japan, there are certain tickets that must be pre-bought. A travel agency can help with reservations and brochures.

AGENCY

Ooh, this looks cool!

If you plan to travel outside of Tokyo and use bullet trains (shinkansen), you should buy an exchange order for a JR Pass.

Got it!

It covers most shinkansen and also all JR trains in Tokyo. First buy the exchange order (with a travel agency) and exchange the voucher for the JR Pass at a JR office in Tokyo after arrival. You must show your passport, as the pass is only available to foreign visitors. When entering and exiting JR trains, just show the pass to the clerk by the window and they'll wave you through.

JAPAN RailPass

JAPAN RAIL PASS

I also strongly suggest that you buy Ghibli Museum tickets. Start looking 4-5 months in advance on JTB's website. Fans of animation and comics will want to check this out for sure, and tickets sell out fast. Tourists can pre-purchase vouchers through JTB (you must set a designated date for the museum visit) and the voucher is exchanged at the museum when you visit. Kids love it!

Life-size cat bus!

With so many great travel website and apps out there, it's hard to pick just a few, but here's a handful to get you started.

WEBSITES

www.japan-guide.com

This site has a lot of great information about different destinations, including rates, routes and train fares. The site is regularly updated with info about dates for festivals and other seasonal attractions. There's even information alerting visitors as to when a given area will be undergoing maintenance or new construction.

www.tokyocheapo.com

This is a great site with fantastic Tokyo tips for travellers on any budget.

www.jnto.go.jp

This is the official site of the Japan National Tourism Organization. It's a great resource for general tourism info. This site sometimes features promotions and contests as well.

www.hyperdia.com/en *(also has app)*

Hyperdia's site shows the routes and the timetables of train and plane travel through/to Japan. I highly recommend using this site to check out the timetables for Shinkansen in advance, especially, if you are using a Japan Rail pass.

Hotels.com *(also has app)*

I find it easy to book and search out hotels on this site. Also, you can get a free night for every 10 nights you book with them!

Tripadvisor.com *(also has app)*

This is a great place to do some more in-depth research on hotels and restaurants before you book. They post tons of reviews.

APPS

Tokyo Handy Guide

This is a great app for exploring the city on foot—great maps and great in-city destinations.

Tabimori

The "travel amulet" developed by Narita Airport. This helps you translate, check exchange rates, check local weather and more.

Navitime for Japan Travel

This app can help you navigate travel in Tokyo, and has lots of other useful tourist information.

Takkun

Really handy if you prefer to travel by cab. With this app you can use your phone to hail a taxi.

Google Maps

Map apps are great, and a phone with GPS is indispensible especially in Japan, where directions can be very confusing.

Tokyo Location Guide

Not what it sounds like, but if you love movies set in Tokyo, this app will point to Tokyo locations where some fantastic films were shot.

Tokyo Subway Navigation for Tourists

Spells out routes and transfers, offers tips on using the Metro.

Good Luck Trip Japan

A nice app for real and armchair traveling—articles, photos, ways to search for restaurants and shops. You can bookmark all your favorites.

Chapter 2 introduces you to:

Suica & Pasmo - IC cards used to pay for train travel and accepted other places such as convenience stores, taxis, and vending machines
Douzo - go ahead / help yourself
Arigatou gozaimasu - thank you
Koban - police box
Doko desu ka... - Where is...?
Hoteru - hotel
Hoteru e ikitai desu. - Please take us to the hotel.
Hachiko - famous statue of a loyal dog in Shibuya

CHAPTER 2

Getting Around Town

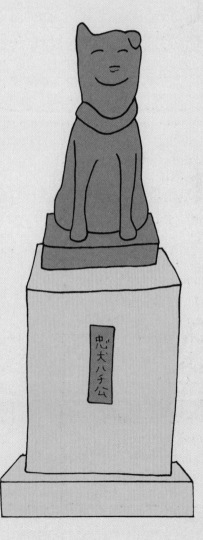

Train transportation in Tokyo is very easy! There are many trains to take you almost anywhere you want to go and usually there is English signage for them. The easiest way to ride Tokyo trains is to get an IC card (such as the Suica or Pasmo). These are reloadable charge cards that can be used for trains, vending machines, some taxis, and convenience stores.

IC cards can be purchased and reloaded at kiosks in the stations. There is usually an English option on the machine. Just look for the "English" button! It is easy to add value to your IC cards using cash with these kiosks. Suica even has a cute penguin mascot!

The easiest way to avoid getting lost is to ask the station clerk which track to use for your destination. The most important thing to be aware of is trains stop running around midnight, so if you're out late, keep an eye on the time!

Which track for Shibuya?

<Shibuya wa nan ban desu ka?>

It is track number five.

Remember! If you are considering taking the bullet train (shinkansen) to Kyoto, Osaka, or another city far away, you should consider getting the JR Pass to save on train fare.

To discourage harassment, there are special train cars marked for women only. Those are designated for female passengers during rush hours. Just follow the English instructions on the signs.

Another courtesy women have on Tokyo trains is pregnancy badges. If you see a woman wearing this tag, it means she is pregnant. Please give her your seat!

What's a Scramble?

It's quite a sight to see Shibuya Crossing, aka Shibuya Scramble Crossing. The lights stop traffic from all directions at once, so pedestrians cross in every spot simultaneously on this huge intersection. People are rushing everywhere, but somehow I've never seen anybody collide!

Getting around on Tokyo streets can often be confusing. I definitely recommend carrying a smartphone with GPS and an app like Google Maps. Often officers in a police box (koban) can assist with directions.

When planning your route somewhere, try to find out which train station exit is closest to your destination in advance. Often the exits are numbered or named.

KOBAN

<Doko desu ka...>

Where is...?

Taxis are easy to get in Tokyo, but they can be quite expensive. You will likely need a map to show the driver. Make sure to grab a map or business card from your hotel to carry with you in case!

Please take us to the hotel.
<Hoteru e ikitai desu.>

Tokyo taxis have doilies inside and the doors open and close automatically! Also, your taxi may be able to receive payment via IC card, so look for an IC card reader.

Whoah!

24

A popular public meeting place in Tokyo is near Shibuya Station by the statue of Hachiko. Hachiko was a famously loyal dog who waited for his master there every day, even after the master died. The statue is a very common place for people to meet up. Everybody knows where Hachiko is!

Let's learn new words with Kitty Sweet Tooth!

Chapter 3 introduces you to:

Otearai wa doko desu ka? - Where is the toilet?

Washlet - high-tech toilet

Ikura desu ka? - How much is it?

Kado onegaishimasu - Do you accept credit cards?

Mizu o kudasai? - May I please have some water?

Sampuru - fake food models, often seen in restaurant windows

Kusuriya - pharmacy

CHAPTER 3

Tokyo Survival Skills

A crucial thing to know about Japan is that there are a variety of toilets! Some are high-tech with buttons on a control panel, a bidet, a seat warmer, sound effects, and more! Or you could end up with an old style squat toilet.

Remember this phrase! Use it to ask where the bathroom is.

<Otearai wa doko desu ka?>

You will see slippers inside the bathrooms of people's homes and other places like spas and restaurants sometimes too. Remove the slippers you have on, and put on the bathroom slippers when using the bathroom. Remember to leave the bathroom slippers behind when you exit the room!

These slippers are for the bathroom only!

Here's a diagram of some buttons you may encounter on a high-tech toilet (aka washlet). It might actually take a while to find the flush button or lever! The flush button could be on the top of the toilet, on the side, a motion sensor, or a button on the wall!

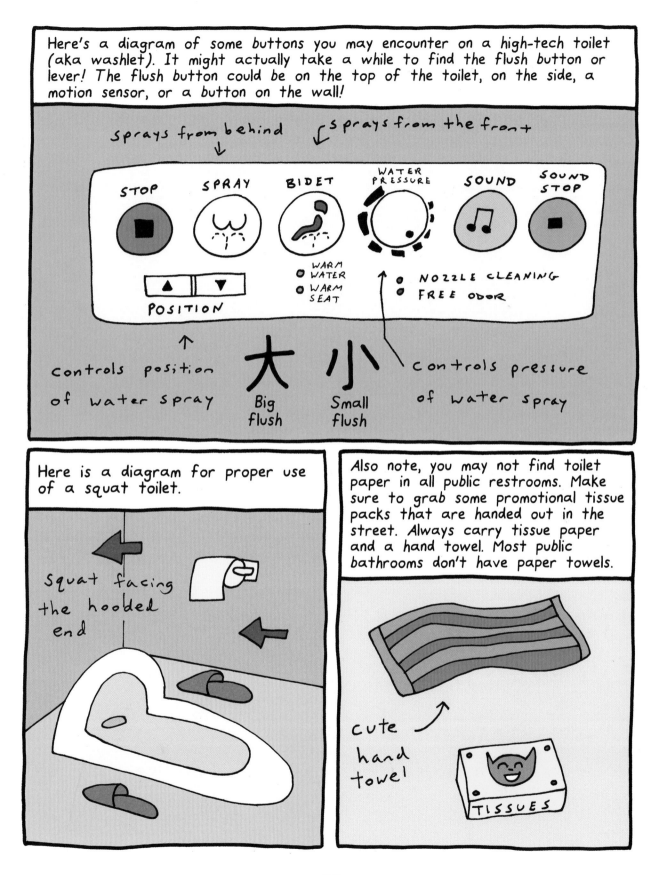

sprays from behind

sprays from the front

STOP   SPRAY   BIDET   WATER PRESSURE   SOUND   SOUND STOP

POSITION

WARM WATER
WARM SEAT

NOZZLE CLEANING
FREE ODOR

controls position of water spray

大 Big flush   小 Small flush

controls pressure of water spray

Here is a diagram for proper use of a squat toilet.

Squat facing the hooded end

Also note, you may not find toilet paper in all public restrooms. Make sure to grab some promotional tissue packs that are handed out in the street. Always carry tissue paper and a hand towel. Most public bathrooms don't have paper towels.

cute hand towel

TISSUES

When shopping and you want to know the price, ask this:

<Ikura desu ka?>
How much is it?

You'll also want to find out if they take credit cards. Many shops are cash only.

<Kado onegaishimasu?>

Do you accept credit cards?

Often there is a little tray you can put your card or money in and they will hand change back in the tray.

Put cash in the tray, change will be returned in it.

Always take your passport with you. Lots of stores advertise discounts and tax exemptions for foreign shoppers. Just show your passport at the counter when paying!

Wow, now I can buy even more KitKats!

DISCOUNT with FOREIGN PASSPORT

When ordering food or drinks, use this phrase: "o kudasai" after the item you want to order.

<Mizu o kudasai.> May I please have some water?

Many restaurants use a ticket vending machine. Just purchase the tickets corresponding to the items you want (usually pictured), and give the tickets to the server. Servers can assist if you are having difficulty.

Yum, ramen!

Some places have digital menus on tablets, and often those will have an English option. High-tech and easy!

I'll have the cheesecake!

Many restaurants will have plastic models of the food in the window - those are called sampuru. They make it super-easy to point out what you want to order.

I can't decide!

You'll likely need to go to the drugstore (kusuriya) at some point, and it can actually be fun to browse in the pharmacies for cosmetics and food. You'll find lots of nice snacks there!

やきいも

137円

Wow, roasted sweet potatoes at the pharmacy!

Here's a pharmacy shopping guide!

Ibuprofen

Hemorrhoid Cream

Aspirin

Eye Drops

Lozenges

Sanitary Pads

Deodorant

Lotion

Shampoo & Conditioner

Tampons

You can get help at a police box (Koban) if you have an emergency.

KOBAN

In emergencies, the phone numbers to call are 110 (police) or 119 (ambulance/fire).

For the U.S. Embassy in Tokyo, call 81-3-3224-5000.

Earthquakes are a fairly common occurrence in Japan. Typically they are not severe. When checking into your hotel, make sure to take note of the emergency exits and instructions in the hotel's room guide. Here are some more tips:

1) Don't panic.
2) When inside, stay inside, and take cover. Get under a desk, table, or doorjamb to avoid falling objects.
3) When outside, take cover if you can. If you can't find anything to cover you, drop to the ground and cover your head and neck until it passes.
4) Keep away from windows and don't use elevators.
5) If in a public building, follow the lead of the employees.

Let's learn new words with Kitty Sweet Tooth!

Chapter 4 introduces you to:

Conbini - convenience store
Gomibako wa doko ni arimasu ka? -
Where is the trash can?
Batsu - X gesture signalling "No!"
Dame - No
Oshibori - warm towel provided
before meals
Maneki neko - lucky cat
Tanuki - raccoon dog
Kitsune - fox
Sake - Japanese alcohol
Torii - gates at shrine entrance
Kappa - mythical river creature
Yokai - supernatural monsters, spirits and
demons of Japanese folklore

CHAPTER 4

Culture Shock Funnies

Japan's Trash Cans (or Lack Thereof)

You will notice that trash cans in public places are very rare in Tokyo. So here are some tips!

Where are the trash cans?

Usually there are recycling containers for cans and bottles by vending machines.

Recycle bottles and cans here

Vendors will take trash back from you, such as wrappers from items they have sold you.

I'm finished with the cone. Thanks!

Sometimes on train platforms you will find garbage and recycling containers.

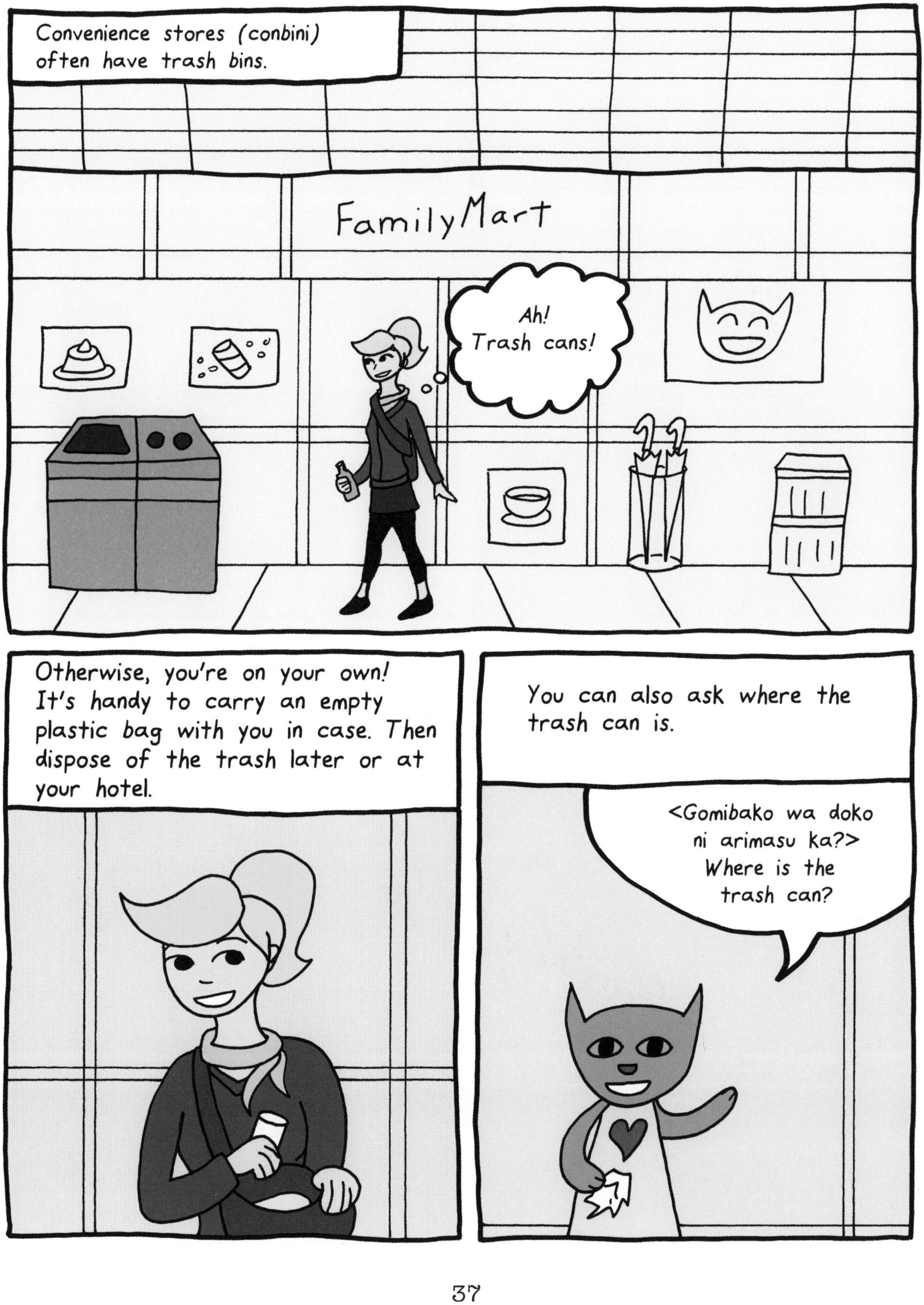
Convenience stores (conbini) often have trash bins.
FamilyMart
Ah! Trash cans!
Otherwise, you're on your own! It's handy to carry an empty plastic bag with you in case. Then dispose of the trash later or at your hotel.
You can also ask where the trash can is.
<Gomibako wa doko ni arimasu ka?> Where is the trash can?

X Means "No!"

If you ever see someone making this X symbol with their arms, it means "No!" There are two memorable times I've seen the X gesture (aka "batsu").

I was trying to dispose of a plastic cup and entered a tourist cafeteria. A woman gave me the X as I tried to put my outside trash in their garbage can.

<Dame!>

Whoops! Sorry!

Another time I wanted to photograph a food stall. The vendor saw me and gave me the X!

Whoops! Sorry!

やきとり

So remember, X means "no!"

Good Napkins and Bad Napkins!

You'll notice there are a variety of napkins and towels in Japan.

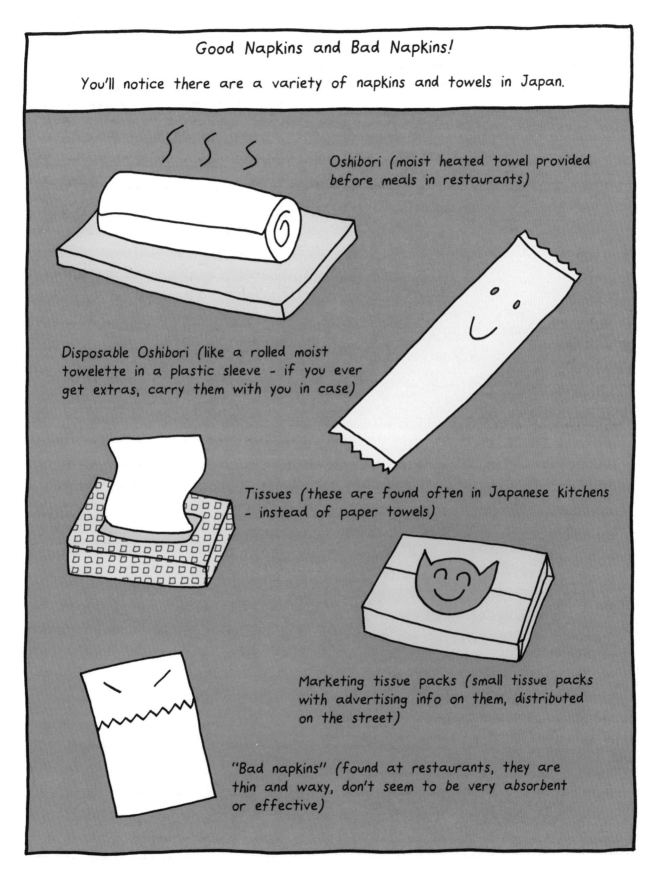

Oshibori (moist heated towel provided before meals in restaurants)

Disposable Oshibori (like a rolled moist towelette in a plastic sleeve - if you ever get extras, carry them with you in case)

Tissues (these are found often in Japanese kitchens - instead of paper towels)

Marketing tissue packs (small tissue packs with advertising info on them, distributed on the street)

"Bad napkins" (found at restaurants, they are thin and waxy, don't seem to be very absorbent or effective)

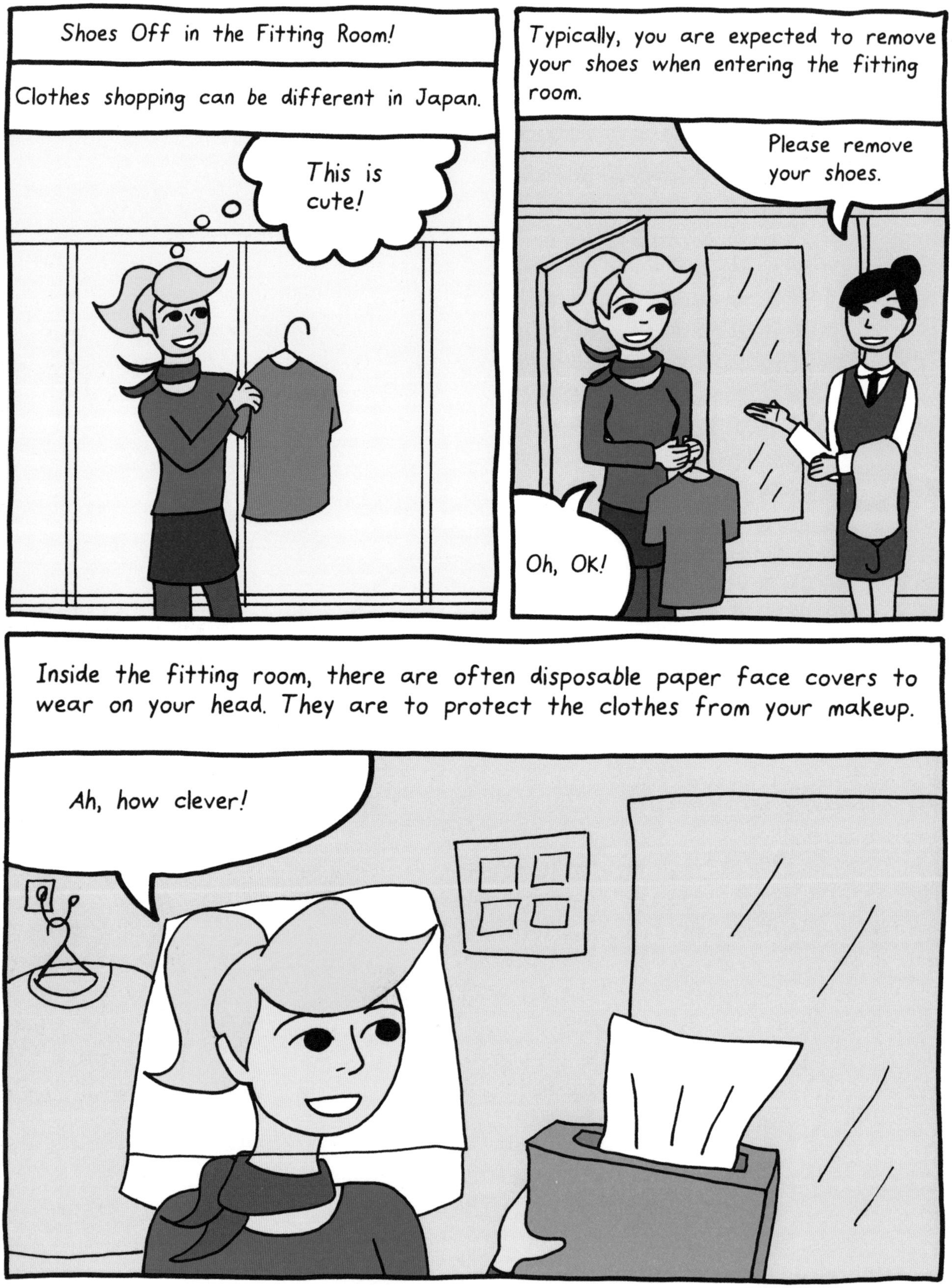
Shoes Off in the Fitting Room!
Clothes shopping can be different in Japan.
This is cute!
Typically, you are expected to remove your shoes when entering the fitting room.
Please remove your shoes.
Oh, OK!
Inside the fitting room, there are often disposable paper face covers to wear on your head. They are to protect the clothes from your makeup.
Ah, how clever!

Tipping Practices and Coin Lockers!

In Japan, good service is always included, so there is no need to tip in restaurants, taxis, hotels, or spas. One exception would be tipping after a stay in an upscale ryokan, in which case you may leave a small tip in an envelope, but don't give it directly to staff.

No need to tip me for service in Japan.

Most train stations will have coin lockers where you can store luggage while exploring the area. They often will take IC Card payment as well. Keep in mind that at busy times it may be difficult to find an empty locker. If you can't find an empty locker, try to find a desk for baggage storage service. Always take note of the locker location and number! It can be very easy to lose track, especially at large stations like Tokyo Station and Shinjuku Station.

Wow, these are so convenient!

ロッカー

Maneki Neko and Tanuki and Kitsune and Kappa, Oh My!

I love seeing the different animal icons everywhere in Japan. Here are a few you will notice.

Maneki Neko

Lucky cats that invite prosperity. They beckon money and luck with their raised paws. You'll see the cat statues everywhere, especially at restaurants! A great place to see many of them in Tokyo is Gotokuji Temple in Setagaya.

Tanuki

Jolly raccoon dogs who wear hats and hold sake bottles! They have humorously large testicles too. You can see them in the animated Ghibli movie "Pom Poko". In Tokyo, you can see them in Chingodo Shrine near Sensoji Temple.

Kappa

A mythical river creature (yokai) that has a beak, a shell, and a damp spot on its head. Often it is portrayed as dangerous to humans, but sometimes humorously too. You can see many kappa images around the Kappabashi neighborhood.

Kitsune

Foxes who appear at Inari Shinto shrines all over. The foxes are messengers to the deity Inari, who represents rice, tea, sake, fertility, success, and prosperity. The shrines normally have red torii gates, and you'll see the foxes standing guard!

Surgical Masks on the Street!

You'll notice people on the street wearing surgical masks every day. In Japan, these are worn when people have colds to prevent spreading illness, and also to filter allergens or polluted air.

It's actually a really good idea! And polite too.

I recently wore a mask for the first time on my flight back from Japan when I was feeling under the weather.

Wow, it's keeping my sinuses from drying out. This can be a real travel game-changer for me!

My mask came with liquid packs, to soak padded inserts; they help keep you from getting dehydrated, and they also are available with scented liquid to make things smell nice. There are also masks with different art and patterns on them if you want to be stylish!

I'm feeling very fashionable right now!

Me too!

Let's learn new words with Kitty Sweet Tooth!

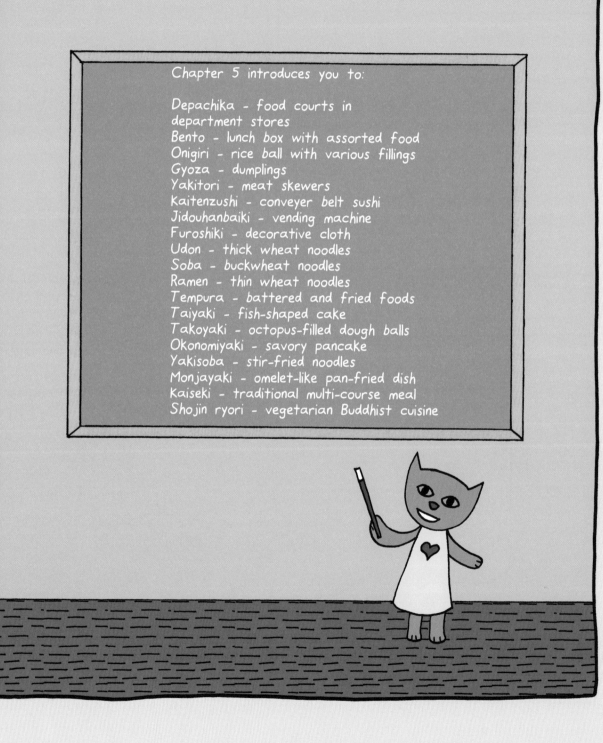

Chapter 5 introduces you to:

Depachika - food courts in
department stores
Bento - lunch box with assorted food
Onigiri - rice ball with various fillings
Gyoza - dumplings
Yakitori - meat skewers
Kaitenzushi - conveyer belt sushi
Jidouhanbaiki - vending machine
Furoshiki - decorative cloth
Udon - thick wheat noodles
Soba - buckwheat noodles
Ramen - thin wheat noodles
Tempura - battered and fried foods
Taiyaki - fish-shaped cake
Takoyaki - octopus-filled dough balls
Okonomiyaki - savory pancake
Yakisoba - stir-fried noodles
Monjayaki - omelet-like pan-fried dish
Kaiseki - traditional multi-course meal
Shojin ryori - vegetarian Buddhist cuisine

CHAPTER 5

What Will We Eat?

In Tokyo, department store basements have food wonderlands called depachika. They are gourmet food courts filled with the greatest delicacies! From fresh bread to wine to bentos, the depachika has it all!

The selection is amazing and you can buy produce, cakes, lunch boxes (bentos), onigiri (rice balls), gyoza (dumplings), and more!

Speaking of produce, Tokyo has very expensive fruit, meant to be given as gifts. You can find melons that cost over $100 each!

The conbini (convenience stores) of Japan are amazing. Usually open twenty-four hours, they carry a huge selection of tasty and affordable foods including onigiri, salads, bentos, fried chicken, hot dogs, and more!

I'll get a nice salmon onigiri!

The major conbini chains include Family Mart, 7-Eleven, and Lawson. Keep an eye out for these logos!

I love shopping for various snacks, like Jagarico potato sticks and cans of coffee! Different shops will have different flavors available.

Tokyo has some nostalgic, retro alleys filled with tiny eating and drinking establishments. Omoide Yokocho (Memory Lane aka "Piss Alley") in Shinjuku is a collection of ramshackle yakitori (meat skewer) shops and pubs. We enjoy the atmosphere a lot.

You can find all kinds of meat dishes there, including horse and whale meat! My favorite was grilled avocado!

horse sashimi
↓

↑
Avocado

And yes, the bathroom consists of urinals in a shared alley behind the restaurants (there is a tiny room with a squat toilet for women). Not much privacy there, so you may want to hold it until later.

Wow, no privacy for the men!

Golden Gai is an area in Shinjuku crowded with many tiny bars. Some are for members only, and many of them can only hold a few people.

We like to go to Cambiare, an upstairs bar themed after the horror films of Dario Argento. It attracts international cinephiles and horror movie fans!

I love buying food at yatai (food stands). Vendors set up stands during festivals and at temples and shrines sometimes. They sell all kinds of wonderful treats!

My favorite yatai food is candied grapes (budou ame)!

My fave yatai food is giant bacon yakitori!

A cheap and easy way to try sushi is at kaitenzushi (conveyer belt sushi or sushi go-round) restaurants.

Just take the sushi of your choice off of the belt as it goes by. The plates are color coded by price.

touch screen menus

chopsticks

hot water for tea

soy sauce

wasabi

ginger

salmon

salmon roe

eggplant

shrimp

At the end of the meal, the plates are tallied for your bill. Some places have a train track that brings you sushi to order via a tablet at your dining station. Genki Sushi is a good place to try this out and they have several locations.

Whoah!

The Wonders of Japanese Vending Machines!

Vending machines (jidouhanbaiki) in Japan are fantastic, and you can buy hot or cold items from them. Hot items will usually have a red mark under the can or bottle. Cold items will have a blue mark.

In addition to soda, water, tea, and coffee, some vending machines carry hot soup, or alcoholic beverages. I've also seen machines that carry souvenir cloths (furoshiki) and toiletries. The machines sell all kinds of things!

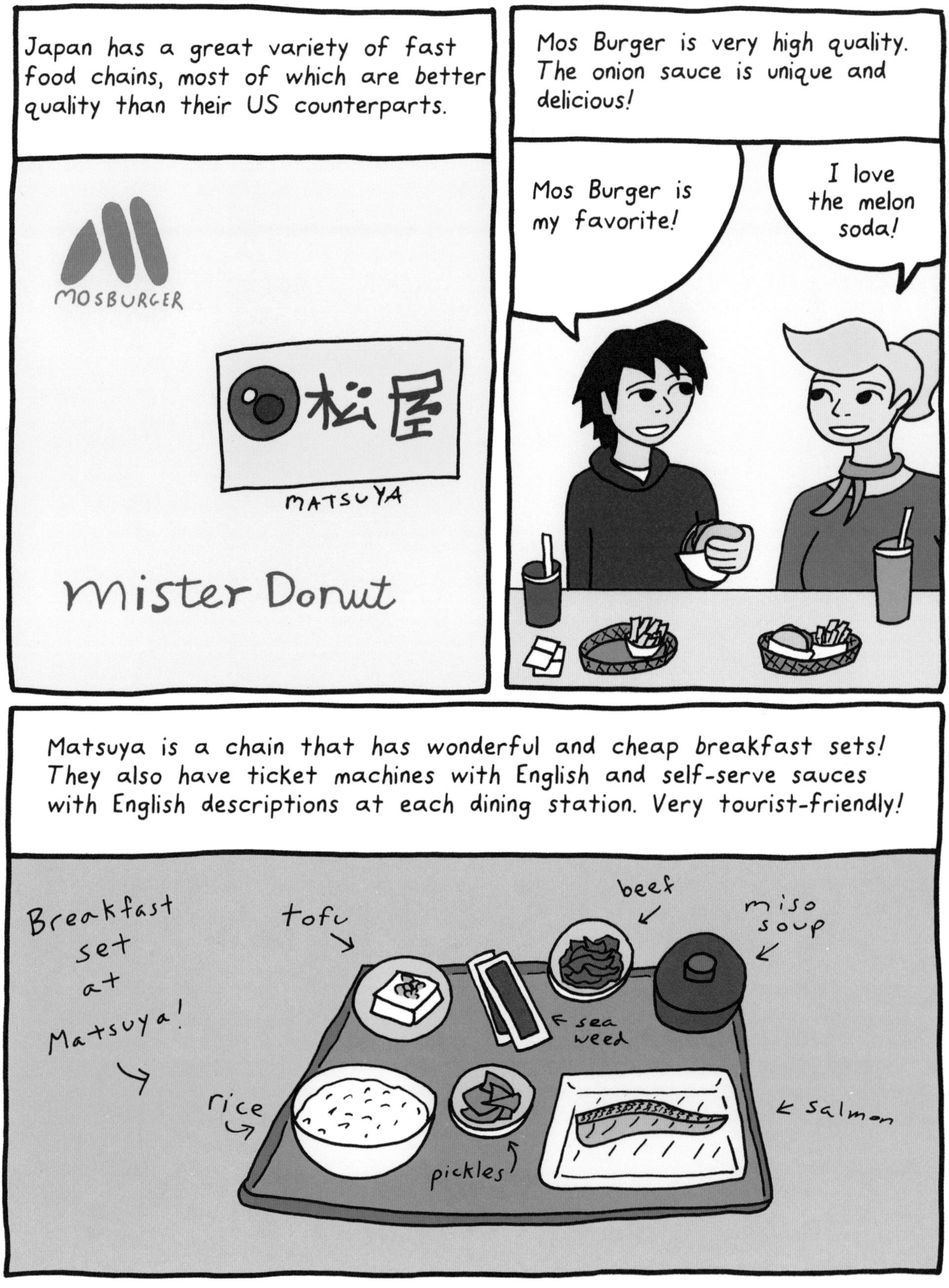
Japan has a great variety of fast food chains, most of which are better quality than their US counterparts.
MOSBURGER
松屋
MATSUYA
mister Donut
Mos Burger is very high quality. The onion sauce is unique and delicious!
Mos Burger is my favorite!
I love the melon soda!
Matsuya is a chain that has wonderful and cheap breakfast sets! They also have ticket machines with English and self-serve sauces with English descriptions at each dining station. Very tourist-friendly!
Breakfast set at Matsuya!
tofu
beef
miso soup
sea weed
rice
pickles
salmon

Japan is a noodle lover's wonderland! The main types of noodles you will see are udon (thick wheat noodles), soba (thin buckwheat noodles), and ramen (thin wheat noodles that can be straight or wavy).

UDON

Udon is often seen with tempura toppings and is very hearty.

SOBA

Often eaten cold and dipped in sauce, soba is so refreshing in hot weather! Soba is versatile and you'll see it in hot soup with toppings too.

RAMEN

Ramen is available in a huge variety of broths and regional styles. Soups are typically salt, soy sauce, pork-bone, or miso based. There are all kinds of ramen trends to keep an eye out for. You could eat ramen every day, and it would be completely different each time!

"Yaki" refers to grilled, fried, or baked food. And there are so many lovely "yaki" foods to try! Here are just a few examples:

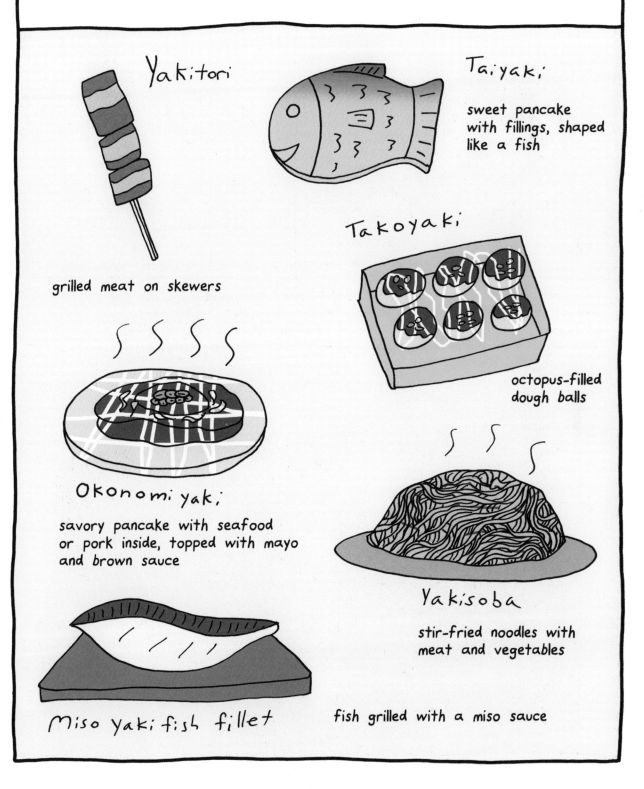

Yakitori

grilled meat on skewers

Taiyaki

sweet pancake with fillings, shaped like a fish

Takoyaki

octopus-filled dough balls

Okonomiyaki

savory pancake with seafood or pork inside, topped with mayo and brown sauce

Yakisoba

stir-fried noodles with meat and vegetables

Miso yaki fish fillet

fish grilled with a miso sauce

Monjayaki is a Tokyo specialty. It's like a cross between a pancake and an omelet and is eaten with tiny spatulas called moji-bera.

The chef (or you could do it yourself) chops and mixes the ingredients on the grill as it fries. It's fun to watch! Many monjayaki restaurants can be found on Nishinaka Street near Tsukishima Station.

Living It Up with a Kaiseki Feast!

Kaiseki is a traditional Japanese multi-course meal. Usually more on the expensive side, each dish is like a work of art, served on an aesthetically pleasing plate as well. Color, taste, and texture are artfully balanced in each dish.

57

Vegetarians Need Love *Too!*

Eating as a vegetarian can be challenging in Japan, as many vegetable dishes are prepared with fish stock or may have meat mixed inside unexpectedly. The best way to prepare is to learn these phrases and research ahead to find the best vegetarian options near places you plan to visit. You can print and carry a card with those phrases or show your questions on your phone to the server so they can understand. Websites like happycow.net provide valuable info for traveling vegetarians.

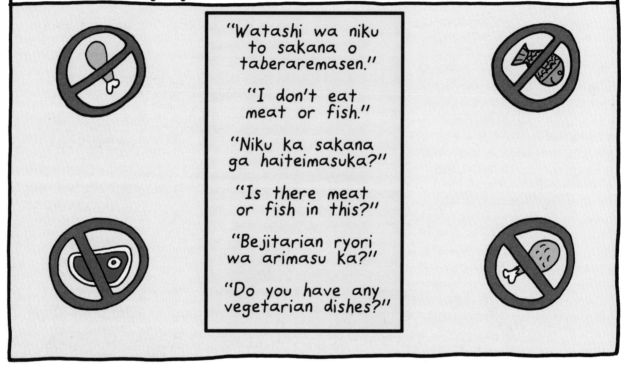

"Watashi wa niku to sakana o taberaremasen."

"I don't eat meat or fish."

"Niku ka sakana ga haiteimasuka?"

"Is there meat or fish in this?"

"Bejitarian ryori wa arimasu ka?"

"Do you have any vegetarian dishes?"

Vegetarians should also check out shojin ryori - multi-course Buddhist vegetarian cuisine.

No matter what your tastes are, you're sure to find food you will love in Tokyo!

DEPACHIKA

Tokyu Food Show
2-24-1 Shibuya
Tokyo 150-0002
+81 3-3477-3111

Isetan
3-14-1 Shinjuku Shinjuku-ku
Tokyo 160-0022

ALLEYS

Omoide Yokocho
7-13-12 Shinjuku, Nishishinjuku
Tokyo 160-0023
www.shinjuku-omoide.com/english

Golden Gai
1 Chome Kabukicho, Shinjuku
Tokyo 160-0021

Cambiare
1 Chome-1-7 Kabukicho, Shinjuku
Tokyo 160-0021

KAITEN-ZUSHI

Genki Sushi (a chain with many locations)
24-8 Udagawacho, Shibuya
Tokyo 150-0042
www.genkisushi.co.jp/en/travelers

FAST FOOD

(You will see all of these chains in many
locations along your travels)
Mos Burger
Matsuya
Freshness Burger
Yoshinoya

KAISEKI

Shunsai
Shibuya Excel Hotel Tokyu in the Shibuya
Mark City Building

1-12-2 Dogenzaka, Shibuya
Tokyo 150-0043
+81 3-5457-0131
A fantastic place to have a kaiseki lunch.
Reservations recommended. (Be sure to re-
quest a table with a view!)

Monjayaki
Many monjayaki restaurants are located on
Tsukushima island.

RAMEN

Tokyo Ramen Street
Tokyo Station Yaesu
Tokyo Station, First Avenue Tokyo Station
100-0005
This food court inside of Tokyo station has
many restaurants so you can try all kinds of
ramen!

YAKITORI

Kushiwakamaru
1-19-2 Kamimeguro
Meguro, Tokyo
+81 3-3715-9292
A popular izakaya open after 5 p.m.
Their meat skewers and potatoes are great!

SHOUJIN RYORI

Sankoin
Tokyo, Koganei-shi
Honcho 3-1-36
Koganei, Tokyo
0423-81-1116

Bon-Taito-ku
Ryusenji 1-2-11, Irya (at Taito-ku)
Tokyo
3872-0234
Many vegetarian options can be searched at
www.happycow.net

Let's learn new words with Kitty Sweet Tooth!

Chapter 6 introduces you to:

Ryokan - traditional Japanese inn
Tatami - rice straw floor mat
Natto - fermented soybeans
Ochazuke - green tea and rice porridge
Yukata - casual robe with sash

CHAPTER 6

Tokyo Hotel Tips

Reserving hotels in Tokyo can be easy via websites like hotels.com, travel agencies, or directly with the hotels. It is a good idea to reserve well in advance, as Tokyo is a popular destination. There are all kinds of choices!

Capsule Hotels!

The most economical choice. Some are for men only, but you can find them for women as well. There is enough space to lie down, but not stand up. Perfect if you just need a place to crash. They don't offer much privacy.

Ryokans!

More traditional Japanese inns, often they include kaiseki meals in the cost of the room. Here you can sleep on a futon on a tatami mat floor.

night shirts

← often no closets

slippers

Business Hotels!

I usually use these types of low-mid-priced business hotels, which are plentiful in Tokyo and other cities. Be aware that the average Japanese hotel rooms are on the small side!

Just make sure to know your checkout time. Sometimes it can be earlier than expected!

Oh, no! Looks like the checkout time here is ten a.m.!

KNOCK!
KNOCK!

10:15

Check if your hotel has a breakfast buffet. Many hotels have amazing buffets with all kinds of choices! It's a good chance to try Japanese breakfast foods. Most Tokyo hotels have vending machines inside and are close to conbini, as well.

Oh, wow! Natto (fermented soybeans) and ochazuke (green tea and rice porridge)!

Most of the hotels I've stayed at in Japan provided a yukata (light robe) or nightshirt to sleep in, and more toiletries than US hotels.

Whoah, a toothbrush, a comb, a facecloth, and nice lotions!

When you check in to hotels, you must show your passport at the front desk.

If you plan to stay for over a week, you might want to choose a hotel that has laundry facilities. Just note the coin-operated dryers can be pretty small and take a long time to finish.

Not dry yet!

Not all hotels will have Wi-Fi access, so try to check that in advance while choosing the hotel, and bring any necessary adapters to connect your laptop with ethernet if possible.

First connect your computer to the ethernet

You can use the computer as a hotspot for other devices

ethernet adapter

(bring your own)

most hotels can supply ethernet cables

Godzilla fans will want to visit or stay at the Hotel Gracery Shinjuku. The famous monster peeks out by the top of the hotel!

Godzilla roars and breathes smoke several times a day!

Chapter 7 introduces you to:

Karaoke - sing-along with musical accompaniment
Manga - Japanese word for "comics"
Anime - Japanese word for "animation"
Onsen - hot spring bath
Kabuki - all-male classic Japanese performing art
Onnagata - male kabuki actors who perform female roles
Takarazuka - all female musical performance revue
Noh - classic Japanese performance art
Bunraku - classic Japanese art of puppetry
Sumo - Japan's national sport of wrestling

CHAPTER 7

Tokyo Entertainment

Karaoke is one of my favorite nighttime activities in Tokyo! Rent a room with friends and sing your fave tunes! Pasela is a major karaoke chain and they have good English language song selections and locations with crazy theme rooms too!

We've used their Luida's Bar (Dragon Quest video game) and Evangelion (anime) locations before. Also, Pasela is known for their crazy towering honey toast desserts. Fun to share with friends!

If you like sci-fi pop culture wackiness, check out Robot Restaurant. With drummers, dancers, battling robots, dinosaurs, and monsters, it's a major spectacle! Make sure to buy your tickets several days in advance, to save money. Tickets are easily available at Tokyo Tourist Information Centers; the centers have locations all over Tokyo.

A robot playing guitar!

A mermaid riding a shark!

Clowns driving robot ladies!

Just a few of the things you'll see at Robot Restaurant!

Another fun thing to do is check out Tokyo's theme cafés and bars. There are all kinds of choices, including cat cafés, maid cafés, butler cafés, anime cafés, there are even horror and prison-themed restaurants!

Kawaii Monster Café in Harajuku is good option if you like brightly colored art and fashion. Each section of the café has psychedelic interior designs by artist Sebastian Masuda, and girls dressed in wild fashions will pose for photos. The food and drinks are rainbow colored too!

There are all kinds of animal cafés in Tokyo. You can dine with cats, owls, snakes, and more!

Polar Bear's Café in Takadanobaba is a favorite of ours, as we are fans of the anime and manga by Aloha Higa. The food is themed after the characters and there are life-sized plushes of the animals dining there! They also have a nice gift shop.

I got the llama white curry!

I got a panda parfait!

Soaking in hot springs (onsen) is a major Japanese pastime, and a fun place for tourists to experience this is at Oedo Onsen Monagatari in Odaiba.

It's an Edo-themed onsen amusement park! Everybody checks their shoes at the entrance and you get to choose a yukata to wear inside. A wristband tallies up your purchases, so no need to carry a wallet. You just stash your purse or wallet in a locker with your clothes after changing.

How to Wear a Yukata

Put on the yukata.

Pull the right side across your chest first. Very important!

The opposite way is how deceased people are dressed for burial.

Pull the left side over the right side.

Tie the sash!

They have a food court, games, and an outdoor footbath that men and women can use together. The main women's and men's sections for bathing are separated.

You are not permitted to wear clothes or bring a large towel in the bath areas (aside from the outdoor footbath). You might feel shy, but everybody else is naked too, so you get used to it. You can bring in the tiny towel though!

You can bring me in and put me on your head while enjoying the bath.

Sorry, you have to leave me behind!
You can dry off with me later!

You must be completely clean before entering the hot baths.

Then scrub yourself thoroughly with soap.

Pour water from the bucket over yourself.

Then rinse off well.

Now you're all clean and can soak in the baths!

It's so relaxing to soak in the onsen with friends after a busy day of sightseeing! Note that most onsens do not allow customers with tattoos.
There are websites to check which ones will permit them.
Tattoo-spot.jp is a good online resource to find tattoo-friendly onsen.

Japan has a unique array of performing arts traditions, and *Tokyo* is a great place to check them out. Kabuki is the most famous. An art that's over 400 years old, it is performed by all-male troupes known for their artful female impersonators called onnagata. Style, movement, singing, and dancing are featured. You can see kabuki shows at Kabuki-za in Ginza.

A more modern performance art is Takarazuka. The shows have all-female troupes with dashing actresses playing male roles. These are flashy musicals with dazzling costumes! Takarazuka are often adaptations of manga or Broadway shows. You can see them at Tokyo Takarazuka Theater.

Noh and Bunraku are other performing arts you can check out. Noh incorporates masks into the performance, and Bunraku is a classical kind of puppet performance. The puppets are beautiful! National Noh Theatre and National Bunraku Theatre have regular performances.

Sports fans may want to check out sumo wrestling or a baseball game. Sumo is Japan's national sport. It originated as a performance to entertain Shinto deities in ancient times. The massive wrestlers grapple, and whoever touches the ground with any part of his body (aside from the soles of his feet) or exits the ring first loses the match. Ryogoku Kokugikan Sumo Stadium is Tokyo's sumo venue; it has a shop and a sumo museum. Tickets are available at http://sumo.pia.jp/en/

The tournaments are all-day events, and attendees with limited time should aim to be there between 15:30 and 18:00 (that's 3:30 p.m. and 6 p.m.) for the most exciting bouts. You can also arrange to visit a sumo stable with guided tours that are offered by travel agencies.

Baseball is incredibly popular in Japan, and Tokyo Dome was the first dome stadium constructed in Japan. Enthusiastic Japanese baseball fans have organized cheering sections and sing songs throughout the game, making it a unique experience. Tickets to most games are available same-day at the stadium. You may also purchase tickets in advance via online travel agencies, or ask your hotel concierge to help you.

77

Manga fans might want to check out Comiket or Comitia, where cartoonist groups (called circles) sell self-published comics. Both are held at Tokyo Big Sight in Odaiba. Comiket is twice a year and features mainly parody comics. Comitia is four times a year and features all original comics.

Wow, there's so much great manga!

Yeah!

Comiket features cosplay, and Comitia does not. There is a designated place for photographing cosplayers at Comiket, so be sure to follow the rules!

To attend, you must buy the thick catalog featuring info on each publishing circle's table. Please note these are not kid-friendly events, as there are many adult comics on display.

COMITIA GUIDE

As you can see, there is plenty of entertainment in Tokyo, no matter what your interests are!

Let's go!

KARAOKE

Luida's Bar (Dragon Quest theme)
5-16-3, Roppongi
Minato-ku, Tokyo 106-0032
+81-120-610-372
www.paselabo.tv/luidas_bar/space.html
(in Japanese)

Karaoke Pasela Akihabara (with Evangelion room at request)
Kandasakumacho, Chiyoda
Tokyo   101-0025
+81-120-706-738

ONSEN

Ooedo Onsen Monogatari
2-6-3 Aomi, Koto-ku, Tokyo 135-0064
+81-3-5500-1126

CAFÉS

Maidreamin (many locations)
http://maidreamin.com/en

@Home Café
Mitsuwa Bld. 4F-7F Sotokanda 1-11-4,
Chiyoda, Tokyob101-0021, Japan
+81-3-3255-2808
www.cafe-athome.com/e

Butler's Café
Udagawa KK Bldg 5/F
11-6 Udagawacho
Shibuya, Tokyo 150-0042
+81 3-3780-6883

Swallowtail
3-12-12 Higashi-Ikebukuro
Toshima-ku, Tokyo
http://butlers-cafe.jp/
(in Japanese)

Kawaii Monster Café
4 Chome-31-10, YM Square 4F
Shibuya, Jingumae
Tokyo 150-0001
+81 3-5413-6142

Robot Restaurant
1-7-1 Shinjuku Robot Building B2
Shinjuku, Kabukicho
160-0021 Tokyo
+81 3-3200-5500

PERFORMING ARTS

Kabuki-za Theater
Ginza 4-12-15, Chuo-ku 104-0061 Tokyo
www.kabukibito.jp/eng/contents/theatre/ka-bukiza.html (in Japanese)

Tokyo Takarazuka Theater
1-1-3 Yurakucho
Chiyoda-ku 100-0006 Tokyo
http://kageki.hankyu.co.jp/english/theater/tokyo.html

LOOK FOR SPORTS EVENTS AT:

Ryogoku Kokugikan Sumo Stadium
http://sumo.pia.jp/en and

Tokyo Dome   www.tokyo-dome.co.jp/e

LOOK FOR MANGA EVENTS AT

Comiket   www.comiket.co.jp/index_e.html

Comitia   www.comitia.co.jp (in Japanese)

Tokyo Big Sight
3-11-1 Ariake, Koto
135-0063 Tokyo
+81 3-5530-1111
www.bigsight.jp/english

Let's learn new words with Kitty Sweet Tooth!

Chapter 8 introduces you to:

Shinto - animistic religion of Japan
Miko - shrine priestess
Kannushi - shrine priest
Kannon - Buddhist deity of mercy
Ema - votive plaques
Amazake - sweet rice drink
Agemanju - sweet bean-filled cakes
Kami - nature spirit/god
Omamori - talisman
GoShuin - calligraphy from temple or shrine
GoShuinCho - book for collecting GoShuin

CHAPTER 8

Tokyo Cultural and Historical Sites

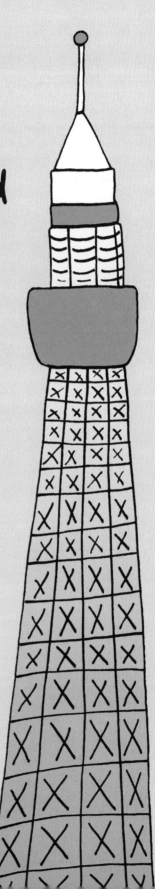

Buddhist temples and Shinto shrines are part of the rich cultural landscape of Japan. Each one is unique! Often shrines and temples will be on the same site together. How can you tell the difference?

Shinto is the ancient animistic religion of Japan, focused on kami (nature deities). Shrines will often have torii gates at the entrance, ema plaques (prayer tablets), and priests and priestesses on the grounds.

Originating in India, Buddhism was imported to Japan nearly 15 centuries ago. Buddhist temples often have fierce guardians at the entrance and statues of the Buddha and of various deities and revered monks on the grounds.

Both shrines and temples will have a fountain for purifying yourself upon entering. Here's how to do it!

1) Taking the handle with your right hand, fill the ladle halfway from the spout and pour the water over your left hand.

2) Then, take the handle with your left hand (refill if needed) and pour the water over your right hand.

3) (Optional) Take the ladle in your right hand, pour water into your cupped left hand. Drink (but do not swallow) the water. Swish it in your mouth and then spit it on the rocks below.

4) To finish, hold the ladle in your right hand, fill it and then hold it vertically, allowing the water to purify the handle. Place it upside down, as you found it.

Meiji Shrine is one of the most famous. It is surrounded by the nature of Yoyogi Park and is very lovely.

Sensoji is a very famous Buddhist temple, the oldest in Tokyo. It's also called the Asakusa Kannon Temple. Beside it is the Asakusa Shrine.

Sensoji also has Nakamise Shopping Street nearby, a lively market with souvenirs and food vendors.

I like to get amazake (warm fermented rice drink) and agemanju (sweet bean-filled cakes) here!

Chingodo Shrine, a little Tanuki shrine, is also nearby!

So many Tanukis!

Another great animal-oriented shrine is Gotokuji in the Setagaya neighborhood, where you can see thousands of maneki neko (lucky cats). It's a must-see for cat lovers!

I'm feeling so lucky!

Me too!

I enjoy admiring the different designs of ema (votive plaques) found at Shinto shrines. Visitors purchase plaques to write their wishes on and hang them up with the others.

I love collecting omamori too. These good luck amulets are available at temples and shrines. They each have specific purposes, such as safety while driving or good luck on exams. They also have different lovely designs, typically reflecting the motif of the location.

We also like to collect calligraphy, called GoShuin. You give a donation (usually 300 yen) and a monk, priest, or priestess will sign the unique stamp and calligraphy of their temple or shrine. Often you can purchase special books to collect these in, called GoShuinCho. Just look for a window with GoShuin displayed and somebody drawing them inside.

Ueno Park is a great spot to enjoy nature, the zoo, museums, temples, and shrines, all in one place!

Ueno Zoo

Kiyomizu Kannon Temple

Bentendo Hall

The National Museum of Nature and Science and Tokyo National Museum are there, as well as the Western Art Museum.

Dinosaur display at science museum

Yikes!

In Roppongi Hills, you can visit the Mori Museum, which features contemporary art. The building has an immense Maman spider sculpture by Louise Bourgeois outside.

To get a view of the city from above, check out Tokyo Skytree, one of the tallest towers in the world!

Skytree is 2,080 feet tall!

The elevator is like a rocket! And parts of the floor are transparent. The view is spectacular!

Not recommended for those afraid of heights!

transparent floor

Oh, no! I can't look!

You can visit Tokyo Tower too, which is similar in design to the Eiffel Tower. The base of the tower also has an aquarium and a theme park based on the popular manga One Piece! https://www.tokyotower.co.jp/en.html

Shrines, temples, museums, and towers! There's so much to see!

SHRINES AND TEMPLES

Sensoji Temple
2-3-4 Asakusa
Taito, Tokyo 111-0032
+81-3-3842-0181

Tokudaiji
4-6-2 Ueno, Taito-ku
Ueno and Yanaka
Tokyo, 110-0005
+81-3-3831-7926

Meiji Shrine
1-1 Yoyogikamizonocho
Shibuya, Tokyo 151-8557
+81 3-3379-5511

TOWERS

Tokyo Sky Tree
1-1-2 Oshiage
Sumida, Tokyo 131-0045
+81-3-5302-3470
http://lang.tokyo-skytree.jp/en

Tokyo Tower
4 Chome-2-8 Shibakoen
Minato, Tokyo 105-0011
www.tokyotower.co.jp/en.html

MUSEUMS

Edo-Tokyo Museum
1 Chome-4-1 Yokoami
Sumida, Tokyo 130-0015
+81 3-3626-9974
www.edo-tokyo-museum.or.jp/en/

Mori Art Museum
53F Roppongi Hills Mori Tower
6-10-1 Roppongi, Minato-ku Tokyo
+81 3-5777-8600
www.mori.art.museum/eng/index.html

National Museum of Nature and Science
7-20 Uenokoen
Taito, Tokyo 110-8718
+81 3-5777-8600
www.kahaku.go.jp/english

Tokyo Metropolitan Art Museum
8-36 Uenokoen
Taito, Tokyo 110-0007
+81 3-3823-6921
www.tobikan.jp/en

Tokyo National Museum
13-9 Uenokoen
Taito, Tokyo 110-8712
+81 3-3822-1111
www.tnm.jp/?lang=en

Let's learn new words with Kitty Sweet Tooth!

Chapter 9 introduces you to:

Gashapon - coin-operated machine that sells capsule toys and more
Kawaii - cute
Sukajan jackets - beautifully embroidered jackets

CHAPTER 9

Shopping for Everything

Shopping in Tokyo can be great fun!
One of my favorite things to do in Tokyo is shop at the bargain stores.
Don Quijote is a huge chain that carries all kinds of items ranging from practical home goods to bizarre novelties. It's also open late into the night. We go there many times on each trip to Japan. Check out the amazing costume selection!
And don't forget to buy a hot sweet potato to snack on!

They have an amazing food selection - it's a great place to find various special KitKat flavors, Jagarico potato snacks, and sakura wine.

Ooh! Purple potato flavored KitKats!

It's also a good place to find luggage, toys, clothes, and spa items like bath salts and beauty masks! Bring your passport to get a tax exemption too!

PureSmile	PureSmile	PureSmile	PureSmile
SKULL	CAT	MASK	CLOWN
PureSmile	PureSmile	PureSmile	PureSmile
		DOG	CAT

These masks are hilarious AND good for the skin!

Daiso is a great chain of 100 yen stores. Everything in there is really cheap (100 yen each, unless marked otherwise)!

DAISO
ダ"イソー

So cheap!

I can't wait!

Daiso is the perfect place to get toiletries and affordable souvenirs like chopsticks, stickers, dolls, food, decorative cloths, and day-to-day items you need during your visit.

Oooh, sake skin lotion!

Thank You Mart is a 390 yen chain store with lots of fun and trendy accessories. It's a great spot to buy socks, purses, wallets, and more. They have a huge selection of phone cases. Everything is brightly colored and cute! There are several locations. I often go to the one in Harajuku.

THANK YOU MART
390 YEN

socks

phone cases ↗

sun glasses

purses ↗

I want it all!

Another good discount chain is 3 Coins, where everything is 300 yen!

3 COINS

It's easy to shop on a budget in Tokyo!

Other fun souvenirs are toys and trinkets from gashapon machines. Gashapon is named for the sound of the cranks turning, and the capsule containing the toy dropping.

GA·SHA·PON!

The toys in the machines can range from anime sets to weird bugs, mushrooms, or funny cats. Some people collect entire sets as a hobby. There's something for everybody! These are perfect for gifts!

cat sushi with backpack

Harry Potter Doll

Pikachu!

If you're looking for video games and manga, Akihabara is a good place to start. Matt likes to shop for vintage video games at Retro Game Camp, Super Potato, and Book Off.

I love Super Famicom!

Manga can be found at Animate and Mandarake. Both shops have locations in several neighborhoods. The sheer volume and variety of manga is mind-blowing!

The world of comics is so inspiring!

If you're looking for vintage toys and manga, Nakano Broadway is the place to go. The mall has manga, books, vintage toys, animation cels, and all kinds of memorabilia.

So many beautiful toys!

Another really fun place to shop is Village Vanguard, which has loads of novelty items and a nice selection of quirky manga and books.

The place to shop for brightly colored, kawaii (cute) fashion is Harajuku. Takeshitadori Street is packed with shops and tourists checking out the wild and whimsical clothes. Takenoko and ACDC Rag are fun shops to check out.

The crepes are yummy there too! There are many crepe shops in the neighborhood.

I got a kiwi and whipped cream crepe!

If you need clothing basics, I recommend the chain Uniqlo. They have cool T-shirts and their stuff is affordable, should you need a sweater in a pinch.

One of my many Keith Haring shirts from Uniqlo

Ameyoko is a great place to shop for clothes, fruit, and other snacks. It has a bustling retro vibe! I love shopping and taking photos there.

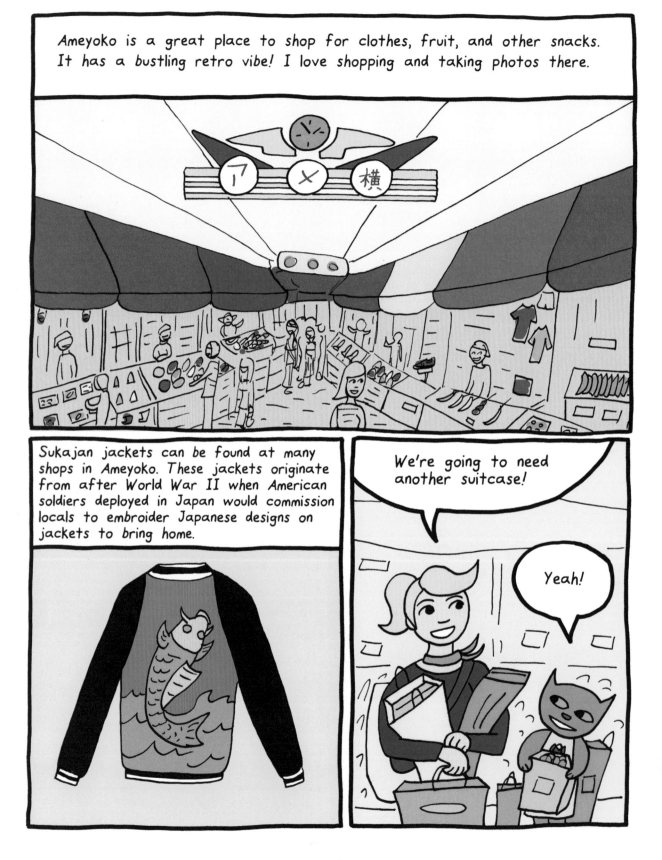

Sukajan jackets can be found at many shops in Ameyoko. These jackets originate from after World War II when American soldiers deployed in Japan would commission locals to embroider Japanese designs on jackets to bring home.

We're going to need another suitcase!

Yeah!

CLOTHING

6% DokiDoki
Harajuku shop with bright and fun clothes.
4-28-16 Jingumae Shibuya-ku
TX 101 building 2F Tokyo
www.dokidoki6.com

ACDC Rag
A funky Harajuku chain (many locations)
http://acdcrag.jugemcart.com

Uniqlo
Stylish, affordable clothing basics (many locations) www.uniqlo.com

MUJI (Nice quality clothing and household basics, many locations)
www.muji.com

DISCOUNT STORES

3 Coins (many locations)
http://3coins.jp/lang/english.php

Daiso (many locations)
www.daisojapan.com

Don Quijote (many locations)
www.donki.com/en

Matsumoto Kiyoshi drugstore chain
www.matsukiyo.co.jp (in Japanese)

Thank You Mart (many locations)
www.390yen.jp (in Japanese)

VINTAGE GAME SHOPS

Book Off
Used bookstore that also carries games, DVDs, electronics and more (many locations)

Retro Game Camp
Kowa Electric Bldg. 1F
Sotokanda, Chiyoda-ku, Tokyo 4-4-2
+81-3-3253-7778

Super Potato
1-11-2 Soto-kanda, Chiyoda-ku
Tokyo 101-0021
+81 3-5289-9933
www.superpotato.com (in Japanese)

SHOPPING AREAS

Ameyoko
The street runs between the Ueno JR station and the Okachimachi JR station stops.

Nakano Broadway
5-52-15 Nakano Tokyo 164-0001
+81 3-3388-7004
www.nbw.jp/#!/en

MANGA SHOPS

Animate* Ikebukuro
(Flagship - there are many locations)
1-20-7 East Ikebukuro Toshima Ward, Tokyo
+81-3-3988-1351

Mandarake* (Akihabara location)
Mandarake Bldg. 6F
Sotokanda, Chiyoda-ku Tokyo 3-11-12
+81-3-3350-170
www.mandarake.co.jp/en/shop

NOVELTY

Village Vanguard (many locations)
http://vvstore.jp (n Japanese)

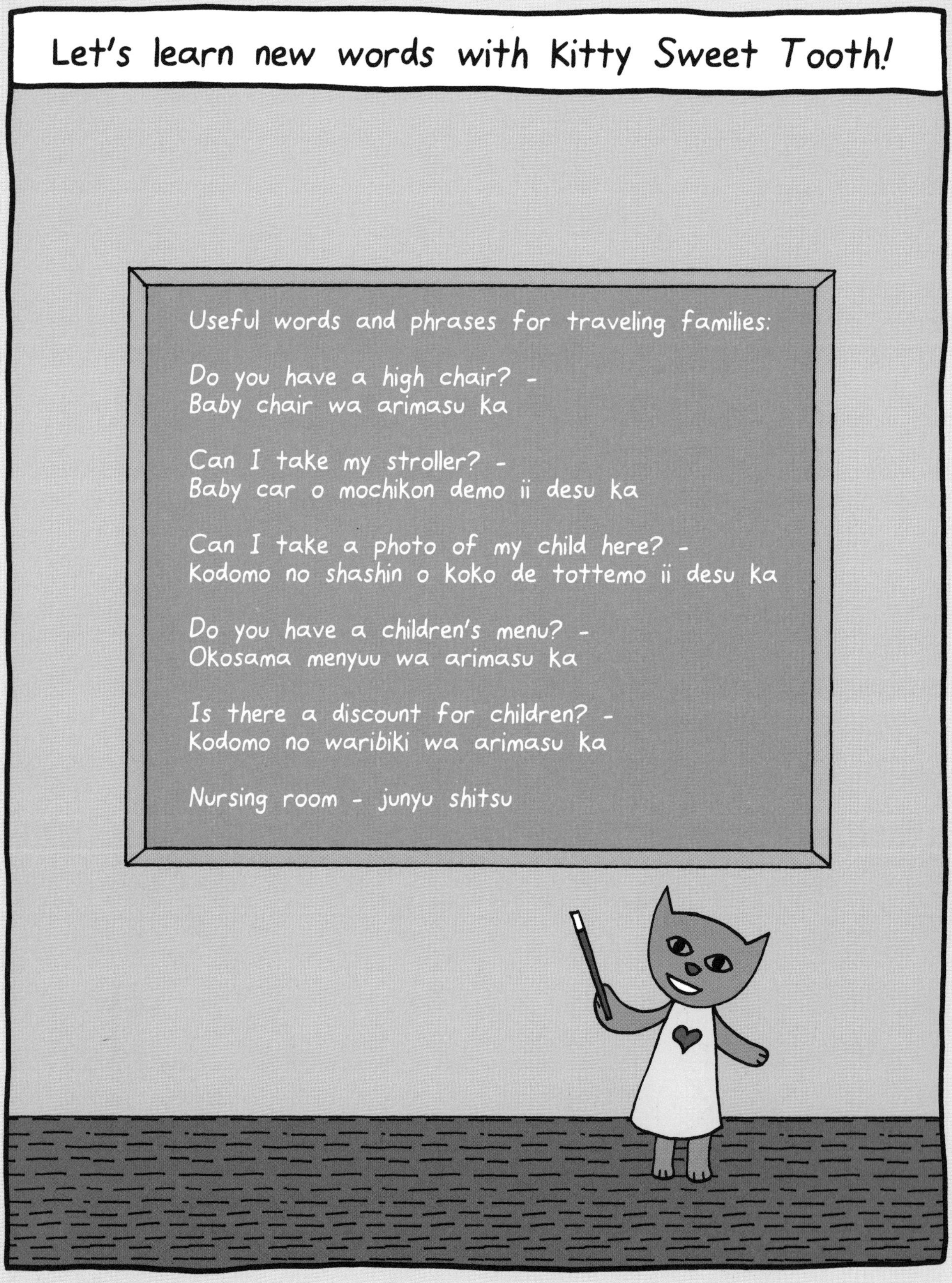

Let's learn new words with Kitty Sweet Tooth!
Useful words and phrases for traveling families:
Do you have a high chair? - Baby chair wa arimasu ka
Can I take my stroller? - Baby car o mochikon demo ii desu ka
Can I take a photo of my child here? - Kodomo no shashin o koko de tottemo ii desu ka
Do you have a children's menu? - Okosama menyuu wa arimasu ka
Is there a discount for children? - Kodomo no waribiki wa arimasu ka
Nursing room - junyu shitsu

CHAPTER 10

Kid-friendly Tokyo

Tokyo can certainly be family friendly. One thing I noticed immediately is that public restrooms typically have a secure child seat inside, as well as changing tables. Also, nursing rooms (with hot water machines for formula) are often available inside department stores.

Baby seat installed on the wall →

Lifts to hold baby in. →

changing table

There are discounts for children to ride public transportation. You can buy children's IC cards (Suica / Pasmo) or train tickets at a ticket office, with the child's passport, for a reduced rate. Children 6-11 years old can get the discounted child fare; 12-year-olds and older pay the adult fare. For children below 6, the metro is free with an accompanying adult. Check when purchasing for current fare policies.

Suica

mo mo PASMO

One of the top attractions for children is the Ghibli Museum. If you're not familiar with the classic animation works of Studio Ghibli, I highly recommend "My Neighbor Totoro" as a great entry point.

Kids will love this whimsical museum. It's set up for exploring, and gives visitors an appreciation for the incredible artistry behind the animation as well. Just remember to reserve tickets with JTB travel agency very far in advance. Start checking their website 4-5 months before your arrival date. If you want to try the museum's Straw Hat Café, go there first thing, as the café line can be long. The museum is located by Mitaka's lovely Inokashira Park, which is worth exploring in its own right!

Laputa statue on the roof ←

Odaiba is a man-made island with many fun attractions. You can ride around it via the unique Yurikamome train.

Palette Town on Odaiba has Leisureland entertainment center and a huge Ferris Wheel. I went there with my friend Mayumi on a Tuesday at 11 a.m., and we had the entire place to ourselves!

Ha! Ha!

Coin-operated walking plush animals!

Palette Town also has a car museum and Venus Fort, a European-themed shopping mall.

Cool DeLorean! Just like in "Back to the Future"!

DMC

Diver City is also a great place to get souvenirs, and they have a nice food court too.

Ooh, sake Kit Kats! And a train-shaped purse!

Tokyo Disney and Disney Sea are also easily accessible from Tokyo. I went to Disney Sea with Matt, and we had a great time! Lots of couples were on dates together and wearing fun Disney accessories.

Disney Sea has several areas themed on different imaginary and international waterfronts, including Mermaid Lagoon, Mediterranean Harbor, American Waterfront, and Arabian Coast. Going midweek is best to avoid crowds. Like American Disney parks, they have a fast pass system. http://www.tokyodisneyresort.jp/en/tds/

My very loose version of the park map!

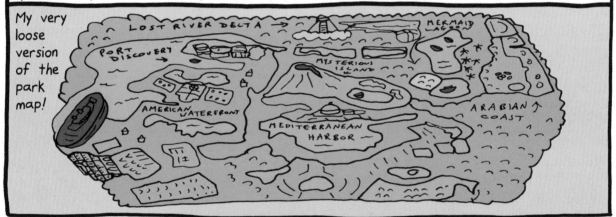

Different park sections have special popcorn flavors for sale. You can get collectible buckets (which include discounted refills) and try them all! Different buckets and flavors are only available at specific locations in the park, so it pays to research what is available online ahead of time.

In Ikebukuro's Sunshine City complex, you can go to J-World and Namja Town. They are indoor theme parks, and most of the attractions are in Japanese. The Pokémon Center MEGA TOKYO shop is in the complex as well. J-World is based on Shonen Jump manga (such as Naruto and One Piece). Namja Town is Namco game-themed.

You can purchase tickets there same-day, and there are discounts for evening passes. Since both of these theme parks are primarily in Japanese, please review their websites before you decide on them. http://www.namco.co.jp/tp/j-world/en/ http://event.namco.co.jp/namja/en/

J-World = Dragonball

Namja Town

Yokai Watch

There is also an aquarium in Sunshine City (Sunshine Aquarium). Overall, the complex is a convenient destination with many kid-friendly attractions!

For Sanrio fans, there is a Sanrio Puroland, where you can see Hello Kitty and her friends!

You're my fave celebrity!

Ueno Park and its nearby zoo are also great attractions for kids and adults, with several museums in close proximity. Fun Panda-shaped treats are also easy to find in the area!

Panda steamed buns →

Panda bread

At Mount Takao, you can see monkeys in the monkey park!

They're so cute!

Fans of the anime One Piece can visit the theme park inside Tokyo Tower!

If you're near Tokyo Sky Tree, you can also visit nearby Sumida Aquarium!

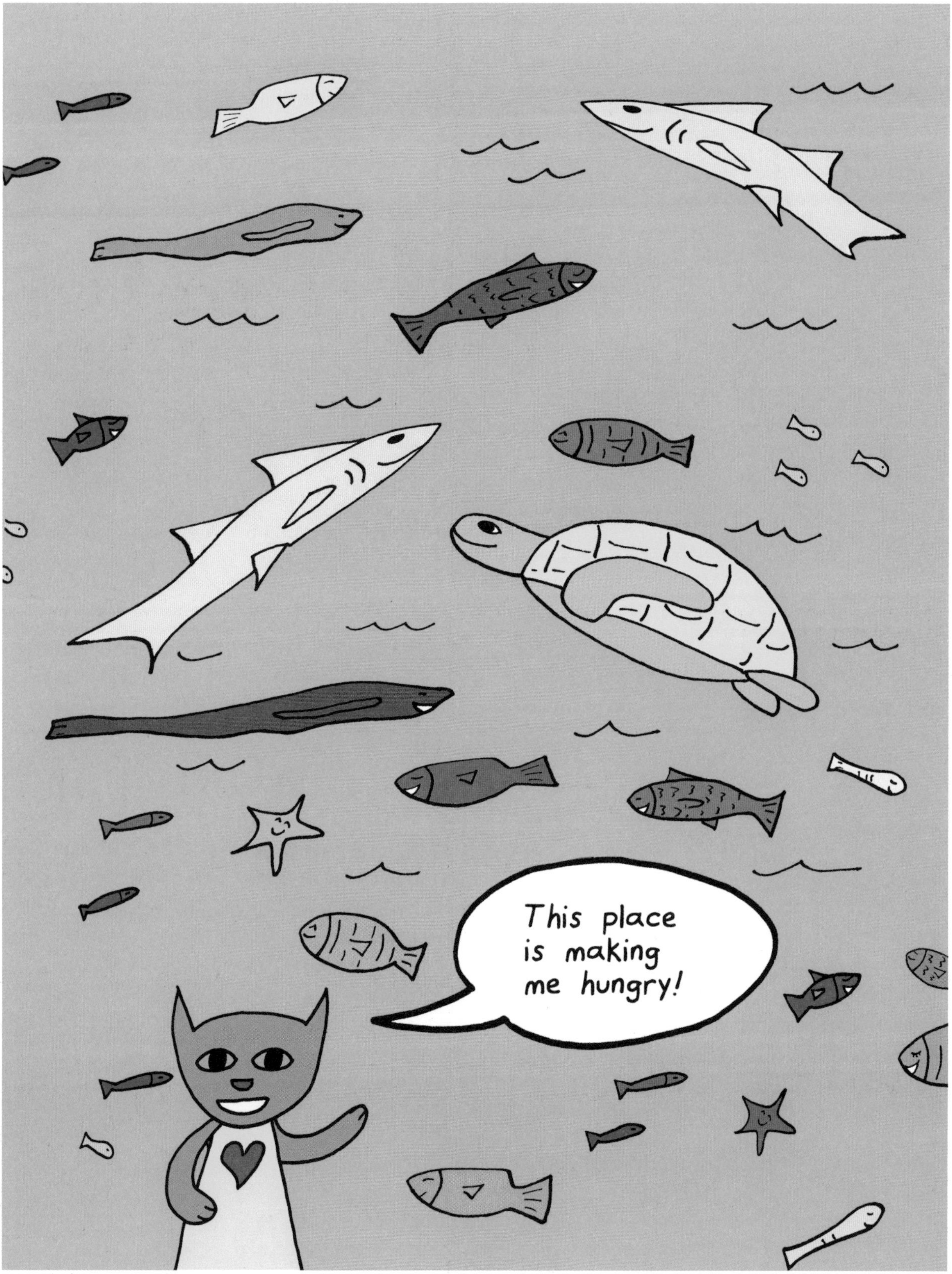
This place is making me hungry!

For kids who like toy cars and other vehicles, the Tomica store has an area where they can play with the miniature toy cars and accessories!

Vroom! Vroom!

Snoopy fans can check out Snoopy Town, the Snoopy Museum, and the Peanuts Cafe. All in Tokyo!

So much Snoopy!

Donguri Kyowakoku and Donguri Garden shops are the places to buy Ghibli toys, and Sanrio stores can be found in many locations as well.

So many cute stuffed animals!

Kiddy Land is a major toy chain as well, with play areas and plenty of toys for kids to enjoy!

KIDDYLAND

AMUSEMENT PARKS

Ghibli Museum
1 Chome-1-83
Shimorenjaku, Mitaka
Tokyo 181-0013
www.ghibli-museum.jp/en

I STRONGLY advise you to buy tickets ahead at this link 4-5 months in advance: http://online.jtbusa.com/Services/GhibliMuseum.aspx

J-World
3-1-3 Higashiikebukuro
Toshima-ku, Tokyo Sunshine City
World Import Mart Building 3F
+81 03-5950-2181
www.namco.co.jp/tp/j-world/en

Namja Town
3-1-3 Higashiikebukuro
Toshima-ku, Tokyo Sunshine City
World Import Mart Building 2F
+81 03-5950-0765
www.namco.co.jp/tp/namja/index.html
www.namco.co.jp/tp/namja/pdf/english-guide.pdf

Sanrio Puroland
1-31 Ochiai, Tama Tokyo 206-8588
+81 42-339-1111
http://en.puroland.jp

Tokyo Disney
1-1 Maihama, Urayasu
Chiba Prefecture 279-0031
+81 45-330-5211
www.tokyodisneyresort.jp/en

Tokyo One Piece Tower
4 Chome-2- 8 Shibakoen
Minato, Tokyo 105-0011
+81 03-5777-5308
http://onepiecetower.tokyo/en

ANIMAL ATTRACTIONS

Sunshine Aquarium
3-1-3 Higashiikebukuro
Toshima-ku, Tokyo
Rooftop of the World Import Mart Building
+81 03-3989-3466
www.sunshinecity.co.jp/aquarium/index.html (in Japanese)

Sumida Aquarium
5-6F, Tokyo Skytree Town Solamachi
1-2, Oshiage 1-chome, Sumida Ward,
Tokyo 131-0045
+81-3-5619-1821
www.sumida-aquarium.com/en

Monkey Park at Mount Takao
+81 042-661-2381
www.takaotozan.co.jp/takaotozan_eng1/monkey/index.htm

Ueno Zoo
9-83 Uenokoen
Taito, Tokyo 110-0007
+81 03-3828-5171
www.tokyo-zoo.net/english/index.html

Let's learn new words with Kitty Sweet Tooth!

Chapter 11 introduces you to:

Dim sum - Chinese dumplings and small bites
Doctor Fish - fish at spas used to nibble dry skin
Fruits Gyuunyuu - flavored milk enjoyed after an onsen soak; coffee or fruit flavors are common
Yuba - tofu skin
Suiton - vegetable stew with dumplings
Jinja - shrine
Kawarake - plate smashed for luck at certain shrines or temples

CHAPTER 11

Take it Easy in Yokohama (and other day trips)

Check out Matt and Yuuko's pages
at the end of this chapter!

Since Tokyo can be a bit overwhelming at times, here are a few day trips that are more easygoing and scenic. One of the closest day trips is Yokohama, a port city south of Tokyo, renowned for its gorgeous Chinatown and waterside beauty. It is about thirty minutes south of Tokyo by train. Yokohama's Minato Mirai 21 harbor features the gorgeous illuminated Cosmo World Ferris Wheel!

In Yokohama's Chinatown, we love to eat dim sum and visit the extravagant and colorful Kanteibyo Temple. Don't forget to buy panda souvenirs! They're everywhere!

That dim sum was so yummy!

Yokohama is also home to the Shin-Yokohama ramen museum, where visitors can sample many ramen styles and enjoy a retro atmosphere. If you love ramen, don't miss it!

Hakone is another favorite destination; it's about one hour from Tokyo by train. Up in the mountains, it is peaceful and lovely!

Riding the bus up the mountains can be scary though! We rode on steep and winding roads in very foggy conditions. Our bus driver was amazing!

We're so high up! This bus driver is super brave!

steep mountain face

Yuuko and I tried out the exciting spa theme park, Yunessun! It was a lot of fun, and a good choice for people who want to try onsen, but prefer to wear bathing suits. They even rent towels and bathing suits on the premises. Also, families can bathe together there. Traditionally, bathers at an onsen are nude and men and women bathe separately, so this can be a more tourist-friendly option. They have hot onsen baths with different beneficial ingredients, like wine, sake, coffee, and green tea!

Green Tea

YUNESSUN COFFEE

sake bath was my fave!

We tried out a footbath with "Doctor Fish." Hundreds of tiny fish nibbled the dry skin off of our feet, and it tickled so much!

HA HA HA HA HA
HA HA HA HA HA
HA HA HA HA
HA HA HA HA

Spa workers occasionally come out and pour ingredients on the bathers too.

Whoah, now we smell like wine!

YUNESSUN WINE

We also went down the outdoor waterslide! It had three different speed slides to choose from.

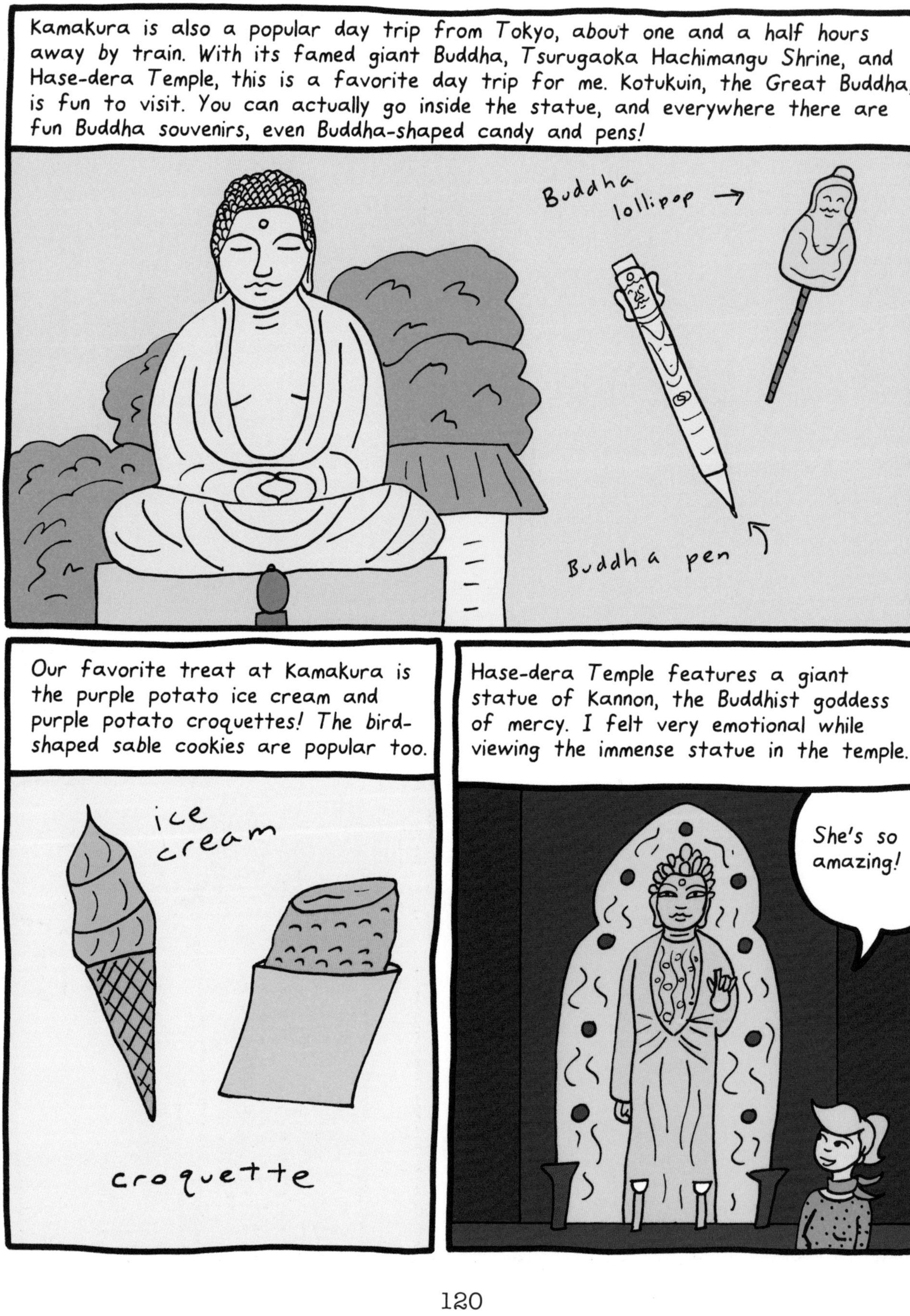
Kamakura is also a popular day trip from Tokyo, about one and a half hours away by train. With its famed giant Buddha, Tsurugaoka Hachimangu Shrine, and Hase-dera Temple, this is a favorite day trip for me. Kotukuin, the Great Buddha, is fun to visit. You can actually go inside the statue, and everywhere there are fun Buddha souvenirs, even Buddha-shaped candy and pens!
Buddha lollipop
Buddha pen
Our favorite treat at Kamakura is the purple potato ice cream and purple potato croquettes! The bird-shaped sable cookies are popular too.
ice cream
croquette
Hase-dera Temple features a giant statue of Kannon, the Buddhist goddess of mercy. I felt very emotional while viewing the immense statue in the temple.
She's so amazing!

Komachi-dori Street is a fun shopping street leading up to *Tsurugaoka Hachimangu* shrine from Kamakura station. We like eating the sausages and other street food while browsing the souvenirs.

どんぐり

Tsurugaoka Hachimangu shrine has a lovely pond with cranes. Locals and visitors put on their kimonos and go there to pray. I got a gorgeous GoShuinCho there decorated with an image of the shrine.

For Collecting goshuin

I also saw my favorite food stand treat there. Candied grapes!

I need to make this at home.

Nikko is another popular day trip from Tokyo, about two hours away by train. It is known for its mountainous landscapes with lovely foliage in the autumn, as well as the intricately decorated Toshogu Shrine and Iemitsu Mausoleum. Several of the shrine's buildings are undergoing renovation until 2024, so check online for the status before visiting.

The gorgeously decorated Toshogu Shrine complex is known for its beautiful carvings. The gilded structures glow in the sunlight! Most famous are the carvings of a sleeping cat and three monkeys.

In Nikko we ate delicious yuba (tofu skin). Yuba soba, yuba ramen, and even yuba sushi rolls were available all over. I also tried suiton from a vendor near Kegon waterfall. Suiton is a vegetable soup with wheat dumplings.

Yuba rolls with beef at zen restaurant

Suiton

Soy milk sauce

Yuba Udon

We went to another shrine called Futarasan Jinja near the lovely Lake Chuzenji, and the shrine had kawarake in the back. Kawarake is a plate that you purchase and write your wish on, then you smash it in the designated area.

We also saw real monkeys eating cookies on a roof! Be careful! They might steal your food!

The bus ride up and down Irohazaka Winding Road can be a bit hair-raising! On a trip to Nikko, you might want to stay overnight, as it is farther away and there is a lot to see, but please note that most attractions and restaurants close quite early.

Another scary bus ride!

There are so many fun adventures to have in Tokyo's surrounding areas. You can enjoy nature close to the big city!

HAKONE ATTRACTIONS

Hakone Shrine
Ashigarashimo-gun, Hakone-machi
250-0522, Kanagawa Prefecture
hakone.jinja.or.jp (in Japanese)

Hatsuhana Soba Honten
(Good soba restaurant)
635 Yumoto, Ashigarashimo-gun
Hakone-machi 250-0311,
Kanagawa Prefecture
www.hatsuhana.co.jp (in Japanese)

KAMAKURA ATTRACTIONS

Hase-dera Temple
3-11-2 Hase,
Kamakura 248-0016
Kanagawa Prefecture
+81 467-22-6300

Kotokuin (Great Buddha of Kamakura)
4-2-28 Hase, Kamakura 248-0016
Kanagawa
+81 467-22-0703

Tsurugaoka Hachimangū
2-1-31 Yukinoshita, Kamakura 248-0005
Kanagawa Prefecture
+81 467-22-0315

NIKKO ATTRACTIONS

Edo Wonderland Nikko Edomura
470-2 Karakura,
Nikko 321-2524, Tochigi

Taiyuinbyo Shrine
Yamauchi, Nikko
Tochigi Prefecture
+81 288540531

Toshogu Shrine
2301 Sannai
Nikko 321-1431, Tochigi
+81 288-54-0560

Zen
(yuba restaurant)
1007, Kamihatsuishimachi
Nikkou-shi, Tochigi, 321-1401
028-853-3470

YOKOHAMA ATTRACTIONS

Kanteibyo Temple
Kanagawa Prefecture
Yokohama, Yamashitacho, 140
Japan, 231-0023
+81 45-226-2636
www.yokohama-kanteibyo.com (in Japanese)

Saikou Shinkan
(dim sum restaurant)
Yamashitacho 192
Nakaku Yokohamashi kanagawa
045-664-3155
www.saikoh-shinkan.com (in Japanese)

Shin-Yokohama Ramen Museum
2-14-21 Shin-Yokohama, Kohoku-ku
Yokohama 222-0033, Kanagawa Prefecture
81 45-471-0503
www.raumen.co.jp/english

BY MATTHEW LOUX

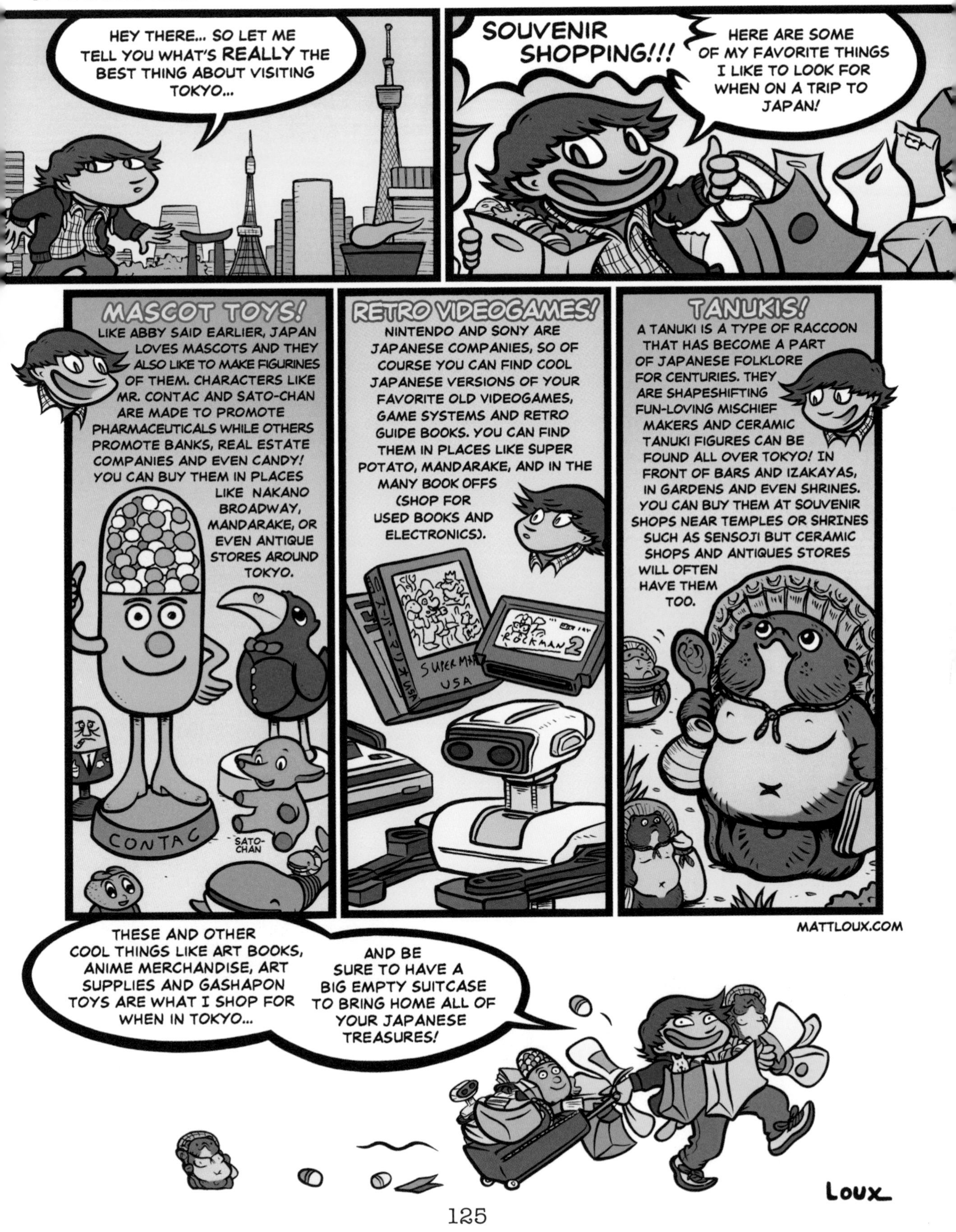

HEY THERE... SO LET ME TELL YOU WHAT'S REALLY THE BEST THING ABOUT VISITING TOKYO...
SOUVENIR SHOPPING!!!
HERE ARE SOME OF MY FAVORITE THINGS I LIKE TO LOOK FOR WHEN ON A TRIP TO JAPAN!
MASCOT TOYS!
LIKE ABBY SAID EARLIER, JAPAN LOVES MASCOTS AND THEY ALSO LIKE TO MAKE FIGURINES OF THEM. CHARACTERS LIKE MR. CONTAC AND SATO-CHAN ARE MADE TO PROMOTE PHARMACEUTICALS WHILE OTHERS PROMOTE BANKS, REAL ESTATE COMPANIES AND EVEN CANDY! YOU CAN BUY THEM IN PLACES LIKE NAKANO BROADWAY, MANDARAKE, OR EVEN ANTIQUE STORES AROUND TOKYO.
CONTAC
SATO-CHAN
RETRO VIDEOGAMES!
NINTENDO AND SONY ARE JAPANESE COMPANIES, SO OF COURSE YOU CAN FIND COOL JAPANESE VERSIONS OF YOUR FAVORITE OLD VIDEOGAMES, GAME SYSTEMS AND RETRO GUIDE BOOKS. YOU CAN FIND THEM IN PLACES LIKE SUPER POTATO, MANDARAKE, AND IN THE MANY BOOK OFFS (SHOP FOR USED BOOKS AND ELECTRONICS).
SUPER MARIO USA
ROCKMAN 2
TANUKIS!
A TANUKI IS A TYPE OF RACCOON THAT HAS BECOME A PART OF JAPANESE FOLKLORE FOR CENTURIES. THEY ARE SHAPESHIFTING FUN-LOVING MISCHIEF MAKERS AND CERAMIC TANUKI FIGURES CAN BE FOUND ALL OVER TOKYO! IN FRONT OF BARS AND IZAKAYAS, IN GARDENS AND EVEN SHRINES. YOU CAN BUY THEM AT SOUVENIR SHOPS NEAR TEMPLES OR SHRINES SUCH AS SENSOJI BUT CERAMIC SHOPS AND ANTIQUES STORES WILL OFTEN HAVE THEM TOO.
MATTLOUX.COM
THESE AND OTHER COOL THINGS LIKE ART BOOKS, ANIME MERCHANDISE, ART SUPPLIES AND GASHAPON TOYS ARE WHAT I SHOP FOR WHEN IN TOKYO...
AND BE SURE TO HAVE A BIG EMPTY SUITCASE TO BRING HOME ALL OF YOUR JAPANESE TREASURES!
LOUX

by Yuuko Koyama

Hi I'm Yuuko.
I'd like to tell you about my favorite dish. It's delicious, inexpensive, and easy to find — **Japanese Spaghetti!**

As Abby said, we Japanese love noodles very much! Along with udon, soba and ramen, spaghetti dishes are a part of Japanese noodle culture, and are growing and evolving the way ramen did in China.

After a big boom of Italian food at the end of the 80s, lots of people had gotten used to eating different kinds of pasta, like capellini or fettuccine, and they came to call all of it "pasta" or "spaghetti." So now people in Japan who call it "spaghetti" are probably middle-aged or older.

"Naporitan" is one of the oldest and most popular spaghetti dishes in Japan. It's a pleasant ketchup-flavored dish that consists of soft-boiled noodles, green pepper, onion, and sausage (which can be replaced by ham or bacon) all pan-fried together.

It's said to have originated from canned ketchup spaghetti that the American military brought in during the GHQ occupation period after WW II. When the recipe evolved, it became the Japanese "Naporitan".

It's still popular as a 20th century retro meal and you can get some — along with drip coffee — at coffee houses.

126

Tarako or Mentaiko (Tarako soaked in hot chili) spaghetti is the most popular Japanese spaghetti dish. The sauce is cod roe cooked with butter or cream. You might be surprised to learn that the butter neutralizes the smell of the fish eggs. When seaweed or Japanese basil is added as a topping, the flavor is one of complete harmony. If it suits your tastes, you will become addicted!

This recipe was invented as an alternative to caviar spaghetti by the chef of the restaurant "Kabe no ana" in Shibuya. Tarako is commonly available in Japan, and cheaper than caviar. Even more reason to love this pasta dish!

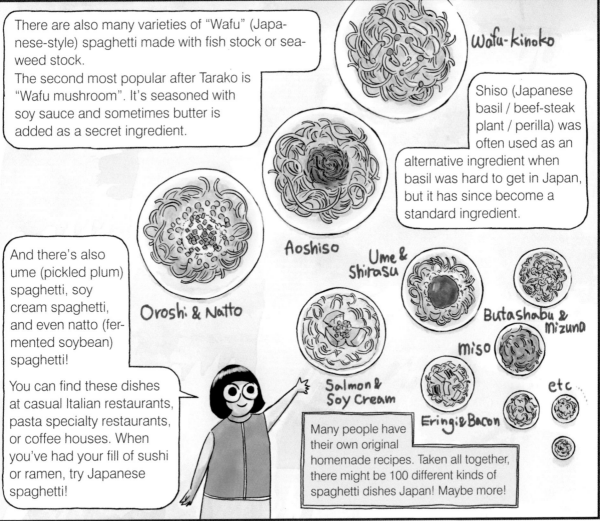

There are also many varieties of "Wafu" (Japanese-style) spaghetti made with fish stock or seaweed stock.
The second most popular after Tarako is "Wafu mushroom". It's seasoned with soy sauce and sometimes butter is added as a secret ingredient.

Wafu-kinoko

Shiso (Japanese basil / beef-steak plant / perilla) was often used as an alternative ingredient when basil was hard to get in Japan, but it has since become a standard ingredient.

Aoshiso

And there's also ume (pickled plum) spaghetti, soy cream spaghetti, and even natto (fermented soybean) spaghetti!

Oroshi & Natto

Ume & Shirasu

Butashabu & Mizuna

miso

Eringi & Bacon

Salmon & Soy Cream

etc

You can find these dishes at casual Italian restaurants, pasta specialty restaurants, or coffee houses. When you've had your fill of sushi or ramen, try Japanese spaghetti!

Many people have their own original homemade recipes. Taken all together, there might be 100 different kinds of spaghetti dishes Japan! Maybe more!

Published by Tuttle Publishing, an imprint of
Periplus Editions (HK) Ltd.

www.tuttlepublishing.com

Copyright © 2018 Abby Denson

Library of Congress Control Number: 2017950583

ISBN 978-4-8053-1441-8

Distributed by

North America, Latin America & Europe
Tuttle Publishing
364 Innovation Drive
North Clarendon, VT 05759-9436 U.S.A.
Tel: (802) 773-8930; Fax: (802) 773-6993
info@tuttlepublishing.com; www.tuttlepublishing.com

Japan
Tuttle Publishing
Yaekari Building, 3rd Floor
5-4-12 Osaki, Shinagawa-ku Tokyo 141 0032
Tel: (81) 3 5437-0171; Fax: (81) 3 5437-0755
sales@tuttle.co.jp; www.tuttle.co.jp

Asia Pacific
Berkeley Books Pte. Ltd.
61 Tai Seng Avenue #02-12
Singapore 534167
Tel: (65) 6280-1330; Fax: (65) 6280-6290
inquiries@periplus.com.sg; www.periplus.com

First edition
20 19 18 17   10 9 8 7 6 5 4 3 2 1   1709RR
Printed in China

ABOUT TUTTLE
"Books to Span the East and West"

Our core mission at Tuttle Publishing
is to create books which bring people
together one page at a time. Tuttle
was founded in 1832 in the small New
England town of Rutland, Vermont
(USA). Our fundamental values
remain as strong today as they were
then—to publish best-in-class books
informing the English-speaking world
about the countries and peoples of
Asia. The world has become a smaller
place today and Asia's economic,
cultural and political influence has
expanded, yet the need for meaning-
ful dialogue and information about
this diverse region has never been
greater. Since 1948, Tuttle has been a
leader in publishing books on the
cultures, arts, cuisines, languages
and literatures of Asia. Our authors
and photographers have won numer-
ous awards and Tuttle has published
thousands of books on subjects
ranging from martial arts to paper
crafts. We welcome you to explore the
wealth of information available on
Asia at **www.tuttlepublishing.com**.